HOW TO CLOSE YOUR CHURCH
IN A DECADE

David Cohen & Stephen Gaukroger

Scripture Union
130 City Road, London EC1V 2NJ

© David Cohen and Stephen Gaukroger 1992
The right of David Cohen and Stephen Gaukroger to be
identified as authors of this work has been asserted by them
in accordance with the Copyright, Designs and Patents Act
1988

First published 1992
by Scripture Union, 130 City Road, London EC1V 2NJ
Reprinted 1993

British Library Cataloguing in Publication Data
A catalogue record for this book is available from the British
Library.

ISBN 0 86201 568 5

Credits
Most of the cartoons in this book originally appeared in
Leadership journal, published by the Christianity Today
Institute, Illinois. The artists and copyright holders are as
follows: *Pages 19, 154, 168, 201*: Doug Hall. *Page 27*:
concept: Jim Berkley, artwork: Gerry Mooney, copyright
1983: *Leadership* journal, *Page 46*: John Lawing. *Page 59*:
Joseph Farris. *Page 75*: concept: David McAllister, artwork:
Rob Suggs, copyright 1987: *Leadership* journal. *Pages 86,
134*: Wendell Simons. *Pages 97, 211*: Rob Suggs, taken from
It Came from Beneath the Pew by Rob Suggs. © 1989 by
Rob Suggs. Used by permission of InterVarsity Press, PO
Box 1400, Downers Grove, Il 60515. *Page 111*: Erik
Johnson, copyright: Erik and Vicki Johnson 1983. *Page 142*:
copyright 1980: *Leadership* journal. *Page 191*: Steve Phelps.
The song by Sebastian Temple on page 220 is copyright ©
1967, Franciscan Communications, Los Angeles, CA S0015.
Reprinted with permission.

All Scripture quotations in this publication are from the
Holy Bible, New International Version. Copyright © 1973,
1978, 1984, International Bible Society. Published by
Hodder and Stoughton.

Phototypeset by Intype, London.
Printed and bound in Great Britain
by Cox & Wyman Ltd, Reading.

Contents

Introduction

The Decade of Evangelism is here. It was first mooted, we believe, by some 'third world' bishops at the 1988 Lambeth Conference. Now, with so much positive talk and activity in local churches about evangelism, we felt that our own contribution was in order. We do not want to see evangelism, or the attendant issues of church life, submerged in papers, committees, synods, and books – of which ours now adds yet another! This book, we hope, will help translate the talk into reality, and will ensure that the frantic activity of many church leaders will be constructive and effective.

The book has a dual genesis. After Steve's best-selling evangelistic book, *It Makes Sense*, and its follow-up, *Making It Work*, Scripture Union understandably saw value in commissioning him to write on a related, pressing concern of his, the leadership of the local church. So, Genesis 1. Genesis 2 happened in one of the many committees David seems destined to attend within SU. He was speaking with great enthusiasm about the varied resources SU has to offer to the church in its evangelistic ministry. A member of the committee, in a throwaway comment, said, 'You ought to write a book about it!' So by the end of that committee, the title and chapter headings had been drafted, giving a sense of fulfilment that not all committees provide!

The suggestion was then made that we co-author a book. It would set out the challenges that face the local church at the end of the twentieth century, and give practical help and biblical teaching on how to ensure that the church doesn't fold up under the pressures but is strengthened, matures, and makes significant inroads into today's secular society. The prospect delighted us both and the task of co-authorship has proved to be smoother than either of us imagined, due largely to Becky Totterdell's patient editorial professionalism.

We come from different backgrounds, belong to different denominations and have differing views on some issues! In very many areas, however, our vision for the local church is the same and our concern for evangelism and the discipling of God's people is shared. David comes from a missionary-pastoral-administrative-parachurch background. He served for eleven years with the Bible Societies in Mauritius, New Zealand and the South Pacific, and Africa, then worked for eleven years in Anglican parish ministry in Sydney. In 1986 David and his wife, Marlene, moved to London and David became the General Director of Scripture Union in England and Wales – an organisation which exists to equip and work with local churches in teaching, evangelism and mission.

Steve is the Senior Minister of Stopsley Baptist Church, which has experienced significant growth during his ten years of ministry there. He is very much involved in Bible teaching ministries with a variety of different denominations, and with organisations such as Spring Harvest and British Youth for Christ. He is a regular speaker at Spring Harvest and is on its Executive Committee. Steve's international links are mostly with the USA – not least because Jan, his wife, comes from Texas. With David, he is concerned to see growth in our local churches, both in numbers and maturity; churches becoming more relevant to the needs of the twenty-first century; radical changes in church structures; and the breaking down of longstanding barriers between Christians.

We hope for two things as you read this book. First, that you will enjoy reading it as much as we have enjoyed writing it; and second, that it will give you the ideas you have been looking for and the encouragement to put them into practice. If either happens, to God be the glory!

David Cohen and Stephen Gaukroger

Note on the structure of the book

Each chapter of the book has two main sections, *The Issues* and *The Way Forward*. By and large, *The Issues* are tackled by David, and ideas for *The Way Forward* by Steve. Where personal pronouns appear in the text, therefore, the identity of the writer may easily be deduced!

1

A Divided Church

THE ISSUES

When I get to heaven, there are lots of questions I plan to ask God. Knowing how many I alone have, I suspect there may be quite a long queue! But then, time won't be a problem there. Perhaps there will even be a special enquirers' department, with a Permanent Secretary. I once read of such a bureaucrat being introduced, by translation, in another language. When re-translated, the title of 'Permanent Secretary' had become 'Eternal Typist' – which might be appropriate if my questions are to be dealt with fairly!

The church = people

One of the questions I'm itching to ask God is why he chose to do things the way he has. I realise full well that his ways are different from my ways, and his thoughts different from mine. But to set up a church with such ordinary people, when he knew it would rapidly become so fragmented and divided, is a cause of interest to me, and of scandal to those outside it down through the centuries.

Take Peter, for example. His track record was not a good one. He'd fallen in the water trying to copy Jesus. He'd completely misunderstood what Jesus was doing when he first refused to allow Jesus to wash his feet. The suggestions he made to Jesus at the Transfiguration – to put up tents for Moses, Elijah and Jesus – were enthusiastic but impractical. His impulsiveness pushed him to slice off Malchus' ear, right in the garden of Gethsemane, and then, despite Jesus' clear warning, he denied his Lord in the high priest's palace.

Not a wonderfully auspicious beginning for any disciple, yet *he* was the one to whom Jesus said: 'I tell you that you are Peter, and on this rock I will build my church, and the gates of Hades will not overcome it' (Matthew 16:18). Two thousand years of church history witness to the fact that this prophecy has been fulfilled in a striking way. And however we may interpret that controversial verse (which itself has divided Christians!), the fact is that Peter was specially chosen by Jesus as a 'founder member' of that church, despite his obvious inadequacies.

The other apostles were no better. Had they been given a psychological profile by contemporary management consultants, they would probably not have made the short list for churches seeking new members, let alone a minister or pastor! Their report may have read something like this:

MEMORANDUM

To: Jesus, son of Joseph, Woodcrafter,
Carpenter's shop, Nazareth
From: Jordan Management Consultants, Jerusalem

Dear Sir

Thank you for submitting the resumés of the twelve men you have picked for management positions in your new organisation. All of them have now taken our battery of tests; we have not only run the results through our computer, but also arranged personal interviews for each of them with our psychologist and vocational aptitude consultant.

It is the staff opinion that most of your nominees are lacking in background, education and vocational aptitude for the type of enterprise you are undertaking. They do not have the team concept. We would recommend that you continue your search for persons of experience in managerial ability and proven capability.

Simon Peter is emotionally unstable and given to fits of temper.
Andrew has absolutely no qualities of leadership.
The two brothers, *James and John*, the sons of Zebedee,

place personal interest above company loyalty.

Thomas demonstrates a questioning attitude that would tend to undermine morale.

We feel it is our duty to tell you that *Matthew* has been blacklisted by the Greater Jerusalem Better Business Bureau.

James, son of Alphaeus, and *Thaddaeus*, definitely have radical leanings, and they both registered a high score on the manic-depressive scale.

One of the candidates, however, shows great potential. He is a man of ability and resourcefulness, meets people well, has a keen business mind and has contacts in high places. He is highly motivated, ambitious and responsible. We recommend *Judas Iscariot* as your controller and right-hand man. All of the other profiles are self-explanatory.

We wish you success in your new venture.

(From *Frogs in Cream*, Stephen Gaukroger and Nick Mercer, London: Scripture Union, 1990)

If we want to hasten the church's demise, all we need to do is focus on the neater, cleaner – structures, organisations, committees, boards and synods – and ignore the fact that the church is made up of untidy, damaged, fallen human beings.

The purpose of the church

To understand the church, we need to know why it exists. The Greek word from which our word 'ecclesiastical' comes denoted a meeting or assembly of people, hence our idea of a 'congregation' or 'a local church'. Some outside looking in may well see the local church as a kind of holy huddle, with a culture and language all its own, its adherents faithfully pursuing a lifestyle that is 'in the world but not of the world'. The Greek word *ekklesia* also means 'called out' Although the concept of being set apart or separate is integral to the nature of the church, Jesus left his disciples in no doubt as to the role they, and subsequently the church, were to play in that world: they were to be salt and light, yeast or leaven – influencing it for good.

It was Archbishop Temple who made just such a point in describing the church as 'the only club that exists for the benefit of its non-members'.

The church was to be a new society, and one with a specific purpose. As John Stott has put it, the church was to be:

'. . . a new human race, whose characteristic is no longer alienation but reconciliation, no longer division and hostility, but unity and peace . . .' (*God's New Society: Message of Ephesians*. Leicester: IVP, 1984, p 110.)

The church is to be the place where all the divisions and hostilities that stem from our fallen nature are overcome and healed. It is to be a community which reflects, and lives out, the reconciliation which its members have with God.

But what is the situation we find? John Stott gives a realistic assessment:

'When we turn from the ideal portrayed in Scripture to the concrete realities experienced in the church today, it is a very different and a very tragic story. For even in the church there is often alienation, disunity and discord. Christians erect new barriers in place of the old which Christ has demolished, now a colour bar, now racism, nationalism or tribalism, now personal animosities engendered by pride, prejudice, jealousy and the unforgiving spirit. [It is interesting to note that Stott omits one of the glaring barriers that still remains – that of gender.]

These things are doubly offensive. First, they are an offence to Jesus Christ. How dare we build walls of partition in the one and only human community in which he has destroyed them? . . . What is offensive to Christ is offensive also, though in a different way, to the world. *It hinders the world from believing in Jesus*. God intends his people to be a visual model of the gospel, to demonstrate before people's eyes the good news of reconciliation. It is simply impossible, with any shred of Christian integrity, to go on proclaiming that Jesus, by his cross, has abolished the old divisions and created a single new humanity of love, while at the same time we are contradicting our message by tolerating racial or social or other barriers within our church fellowship.' (John Stott, *God's New Society*.)

Barriers

Barriers. The very things that Christ came to destroy are being perpetuated among those who call themselves his followers. Not only are there barriers between the church and the world, hindering the world from believing in Jesus, but the offences of division are found within the church itself, often perpetuated by a colluding congregation. Let's look at some of these barriers and at what it is that maintains them.

Clericalism

The lay-clerical divide is one of the most widely accepted barriers. It is thought to be normal and now even traditional Brethren congregations are increasingly moving towards employing full-time teaching elders. Of course, the pastor, minister, elder or whatever does play a vital role, but in reality there is all too often a collar bar, encouraged both by some clergy and some laity. The former either enjoy the power which they can gain from their role or else feel a misguided responsibility to assume a priestly function. The latter believe the minister is 'the professional', trained and paid to do the task of ministry, thereby relieving the 'lay' person of responsibility and involvement. But the people of God, the *laos* or laity, are meant to be one, acting together in all the work of ministry and worship, which is why the Protestant reformers went to the stake on the issue of the priesthood of all believers.

Paul, when he wrote to the churches in Galatia, was painting the same picture, but on an even broader canvas. For those who are 'in Christ' (surely the church by any definition), 'there is neither Jew nor Greek, slave nor free, male nor female, for you are all one in Christ Jesus' (Galatians 3:28).

The last phrase has flown proudly above Keswick Convention platforms in many parts of the world for a century or more. But the church it describes is as fragmented as ever by the racial, class and gender distinctions Paul was abhorring in this classic statement.

Racism

'There is neither Jew nor Greek.' This claim would have

11

astounded those who first heard it. The overtones in Paul's day were as much cultural as racial, but the application to our race-conscious culture is as relevant as ever.

The phenomenon of so-called 'black-led churches' in England would never have happened had the indigenous church in the 1950s and 1960s been true to its calling. Many committed church members arrived 'home' from Britain's former colonies, only to be cold-shouldered by the very community they had expected to welcome them. Black Christians were forced to set up their own congregations. Now, the life and growth of such congregations, particularly in urban areas, makes dwindling white churches think wistfully about opportunities that were lost.

Despite valiant attempts, little has changed. Is it because of the unwillingness of many to adapt to the cultural changes that would make non-WASPS (White Anglo-Saxon Protestants) welcome? Or is it a more reprehensible, ingrained racism that none of us who follow Christ would wish to own, but may need to confess?

'Classism'

'There is . . . neither slave nor free.' In its cultural context, this spoke to the Galatians of the kind of class distinction that James highlighted in his letter when he urged his readers not to show favouritism (James 2:1). It is an observable fact, at least in the wealthy western world, that the church has made few inroads into the working classes, or into the aristocracy. It has been caricatured in England, as 'the Tory party at prayer'.

Such descriptions are, of course, generalisations. In the 'two-thirds third world', where the church is growing most rapidly, numerically, it is mainly in the poorest sectors of society that the impact is being felt. Africa and Latin America provide good examples of this.

It also has to be said that some church growth theorists favour what has been called the 'homogeneous unit principle', which states that church growth is more likely to happen when congregations are of a kind, be it social stratum, race, occupation, or language.

The fact remains that most congregations happen to fit the

homogeneous description, more by nature than design. Some readers may well feel this is not so, because their current experience is different, with a well mixed congregation that reflects the biblical ideal. But the overall picture does not reflect this.

Sexism

'There is . . . neither male nor female.' Recently, a heightened awareness of the barrier of sexism in the church has resulted in a plethora of books on the subject, adding fuel to the fire of polarisation that Paul was wanting the church to avoid. Statistically, the human population is approximately balanced between male and female, with slight weighting in favour of women. In the church, women attending and participating vastly outnumber the men; while in leadership, the reverse is true, to the increasing chagrin of women and the embarrassment of increasing numbers of men.

There are strong traditional and historical reasons for this imbalance, and one has to respect the strongly held principles of those who urge, for example, that 'leadership is male', as David Pawson does. (His argument is set out in his book, *Leadership is Male*. Crowborough: Highland Books, 1988.)

The fundamental issue goes back to creation. Both sides of the debate agree that what God made at creation was good at each stage, reaching the pinnacle when male and female were created. Each was created in God's image and 'it was very good' (Genesis 1:27, 31).

Then came the fall, as a result of humankind's wilful disobedience. The human saga fills the pages of the Bible until Christ comes and lives, teaches, suffers and dies – for what purpose? To redeem what was lost at the fall, that mutuality of shared dominion God gave to Adam and Eve. To suggest anything less, undermines the effect of the Cross and leaves us living defeated lives, still in the shadow of the fall, rather than in that new society Stott was describing from Ephesians.

To use Genesis 3 to bolster male dominion misses the point that that chapter is *descriptive* of what was to happen as a result of sin, and not *prescriptive* of God's plan for his people, his church.

A sad travesty of biblical understanding surfaced in one of

the churches in which we ministered in Australia. After a radical conversion had transformed the lives of a young couple from a hippy life-style to a conservative Christian one, the emphasis on male leadership led to unexpected consequences. A list of duties was placed on the refrigerator door each morning, which the husband expected his wife to have performed by the time he returned that evening.

Needless to say, such behaviour was the tip of an iceberg, indicating more serious underlying problems that ultimately destroyed both the relationship and the marriage. The sad fact was that the Bible was used to bolster such obviously unbiblical attitudes and behaviour – as it is whenever the divisions of race, class or gender are perpetuated in God's name.

How, then, can we close our church in a decade? A good way to begin would be to *reject* all those who, though 'in Christ', are different from ourselves – perhaps in temperament, background, understanding, or with different preferences in worship and spirituality. We perpetuate divisions and delight in applying labels to all and sundry, indicating by their use that others are not like us. But God has a purpose in making the body of Christ infinitely rich in its variety. May God preserve us from thinking everyone else should be like us! What a boring place it would be!

A second way to close the church quickly would be to go to the other extreme and *ignore* the differences between us, stifling the variety of gifts God has given to his people. A good way to do this is to ensure that everything depends on the man out front. There can be no untidy clashes of personality or style then! In our last church, we wanted to make it clear that we did not regard the minister as having all the gifts needed for ministry, so when listing staff members in the weekly news sheet we put:

'Ministers: every member of the congregation.' (It was not an original idea, but one borrowed from Terry Fullam.)

How can we get the balance right – on the one hand trying to draw together as the reconciled body of Christ; but on the other, not squashing and ignoring our distinctives?

14

THE WAY FORWARD

No one watching television during November 1989 will forget those first steps in dismantling the Berlin Wall, nor the tears of joy from East and West Germans alike. Over the last ten years we have seen many of these 'Berlin Walls' in the church of Jesus begin to be taken down: the 'wall' between clergy and laity, different cultures, races and classes, and men and women.

While we praise God for this, we are forced to admit that the demolition process is often painfully slow. In fact, there are those who seem intent on putting the walls back up as quickly as they are coming down! How can local churches get involved in breaking down, *and keeping down*, these 'walls of division'? This question helps keep us honest. Unless individual Christians and local churches change their behaviour, any number of denominational resolutions, well argued books or high-powered conferences will not succeed in breaking these barriers down.

Before jumping on a spiritual bulldozer, churches should acknowledge the size of the walls! Any successful demolition job will have to take these factors into account:

● *It takes time.* Rome wasn't built over a bank holiday weekend. Barriers which have taken years to erect (sometimes centuries!) won't fall down easily.

● *People's feelings, attitudes and convictions.* Some of the bricks are made of people's feelings, attitudes, even deeply held convictions. They need to be taken down with care. Keep in mind that you want to destroy the *wall* not the *bricks*! After all, you may need them to build a church!

● *People's sense of security.* These walls sometimes represent people's security. Don't try to demolish all the wall in one go! Often, folk are more willing to join in the dismantling when the top few rows are taken off and they can see that the view on the other side is not as threatening as they thought it was!

With these cautions in mind, we'll go on to look at the specific barriers we have already mentioned.

Professionals versus amateurs?

In the divide between ordained clergy – the 'professionals' – and lay Christians, a change of attitude is needed on both sides. Church leaders, whether known as ministers, vicars, elders or anything else, need to loosen their hold on their ministries, become less protective about the privileges of their position and start acting on their belief in 'every member ministry'. At the same time, though, church members need to stop putting the clergy on a pedestal marked 'omnicompetent' or in a box marked 'the bit of the church that does the work' and start acting on *their* belief in every member ministry!

In practice, in most local fellowships of Christians it is the leaders who must initiate the tearing down of the walls. Over the last decade this has been happening in our churches, and it needs to continue if the full benefits are to be reaped.

Shared leadership is a crucial step in this process. The establishment of an eldership, the redefining of the role of deacon, adding other 'staff' members, the review of committee functions – these can all lead to the involvement of others in the authority and responsibility structures of the church. Of course churches need a leader, probably a strong one; but not at the cost of stifling the leadership skills of others in the body of Christ.

Making changes

As leaders embark on this journey they will need to keep those in the current leadership structures informed of what is being planned and why, in order to keep petty jealousies and insecurities to a minimum. *Information* and *explanation* are the two vital steps that must precede gentle *implementation*. While this formal process continues, the leader needs to be developing the idea 'informally'. Of course he can preach through the appropriate biblical material (eg 1 Corinthians 12; Ephesians 4:1–16) and ensure the discussion of these ideas in study groups, or provide more relaxed opportunities for feedback – perhaps over coffee in the church hall. But he also needs to be looking actively for those whom God may be calling to share in leadership – from both inside and outside the current leadership structures. The place of prayer cannot be over-emphasised in all this. Too often the whole process simply degenerates into 'looking for clever people' or worse, merely elevating into positions of authority people you happen to like and get on well with! This issue must have the stamp of God on it or we will simply replace a one-person dictatorship with an equally authoritarian oligarchy or (at the other extreme) an unmanageable, muddled democracy, where everyone does what is right in his or her own eyes!

God's Spirit wants to produce a thoroughly biblical church leadership where godly people share responsibility, where titles mean less than functions and where the common goal is the growth of God's kingdom; a leadership which takes both the needs of the people and its own understanding of the biblical mandates very seriously.

Problems!

Of course, the fact is that many churches have gone down this route only to discover major difficulties! Sharing leadership sounds all very good, but in practice a number of tensions have slowed us down.

• *People are a pain!* Shared leadership stops giving you a warm glow when people disagree with you. In the early years you may obtain agreement by dint of friendship, personality or the old patterns of 'agreeing with the minister', continuing in the new structure. Sooner or later someone is going to disagree with you if only to find out whether your new commitment to sharing your leadership is cosmetic or real!

• *Everything takes longer!* Or at least it seems to. Other people now have a view on things and they expect to be taken seriously. This means consultation and discussion . . . or hurt can result. Many a minister has appointed an eldership hoping to share responsibility and work-load but has ended up *creating* additional work and sharing only his privileges!

• *Standards fall!* Other people just may not be as good as you are at leading meetings, making good decisions or handling some of the responsibilities of leadership. And why should they be? How well would you handle *their* work

17

situation if you were plunged into it with only a twenty-minute chat and a quick prayer to help you?

Many churches in Britain are at this stage of development – committed to change but struggling with the tensions. These tensions can be so bad that at times the whole process is called into question. 'The old way was bad but was it *this* bad?' After all the emphasis on shared leadership in the 1970s and 1980s – its importance and how to make it work – it seems as though, with the 1990s, we've ended up in a bit of a desert. Many church leaders appear to be looking for refreshment and fruitfulness in a wilderness of unfulfilled expectations, thwarted desires and conflicting priorities. Just as it did to God's people of old, 'Egypt' looks pretty inviting when compared with the insecurities and conflicts of the wilderness. I am convinced that large numbers of churches will, in this decade, have to make a deliberate decision: retreat to the Egypt of one-man leadership, or make a costly, further advance into the promised land. Sadly, I fear, some will opt for Egypt.

For others, the steady, though often unspectacular progress will continue and it will have its impact not simply on leadership structures but on every aspect of church life. We will have to continue to be open to new ideas, ready to admit it when we get it wrong and take every opportunity to put into practice those things which tear down the barriers between the (so called) laity and (so called) clergy.

Freeing gifts and ministries
Probably the crucial area in implementing these changes is recognising gifts and ministries. On a purely human level we ought to recognise that lots of people in the church have abilities which the leader does not. What's more, there are more of them! Better to get ten people working than to do the work of ten people. For too long the church has been like the scene at a professional football match – thousands of people who desperately need exercise watching twenty-two who desperately need rest! Progress is slower initially when you use other people but in the long term it makes growth of all kinds both possible and sustainable.

'My wife, Anita, will be contributing to my sermon, "Candour in the Christian Home."'

On the supernatural level, it is the body of Christ which contains all the spiritual gifts, not the body of the vicar! These gifts should be identified, encouraged and released in the life of the fellowship. Here are some ways of working this out practically:

• *Encourage contributions to public worship.* What a release some churches have known through inviting different members of the congregation to read scripture, lead in prayer, preach, play an instrument or give testimony to an answer to prayer!

• *Encourage 'unplanned' contributions to public worship.* Times to share 'a word from the Lord', pray spontaneously or read a Bible verse can be valuable. Allow a chance for questions after the sermon (or during it?!). Perhaps far more of our services should have some element which is not 'controlled' from the front.

• *Encourage participation in communion and baptism.* Share these responsibilities around. Many leaders (myself included) have known the joy of sharing the task of baptising others.

• *Reassess the leader's tasks.* Is the leader the best person to chair meetings? If other people would do it better than him, why don't they? What else is he doing for which he feels

19

neither called nor gifted? Can these things be done by others?

● *Make sure the leader is not present at every meeting of the church*. Whatever is *said* about every member ministry, very few people will believe it if the leader(s) demonstrate(s) the opposite.

The battle of the sexes

For many non-Christians, the way the church appears to treat women is a major stumbling block to their coming to faith. Whatever the rights and wrongs theologically about women's ordination and the role of women in leadership generally, there can be little doubt that we are viewed by the world as anachronistic, even obscurantist, in this area.

In our response to this, we seem to be polarising within the church. Put crudely, there is either a reversion to a chauvinism which seems to be trying to set the clock back a hundred years or a wholesale acceptance of a feminism which owes more to Greer and Steinam (of 'a woman without a man is like a fish without a bicycle' fame) than to Jesus or Paul.

Neither of these positions seem to offer a biblical, practical way forward into the nineties. Let me describe four positive responses a local church can make to this issue in an attempt to begin to break down this barrier between the sexes.

1 Repentance

It is hard to get away from the need for repentance. The male-dominated church seems to have taken on board from the male-dominated British culture over the last few centuries, many negative views of women. We have, of course, bolstered these ideas with appropriate biblical verses and rested on the assumption that we were merely applying a divine distinction between men and women. Even if this view were right, church authorities have been far from consistent. While maintaining this distinction at *home* we have happily sent women *abroad* to preach, teach and plant churches; sometimes in conditions of the most awful danger and appalling squalor. Here is hypocrisy on a monumental scale! No wonder Christian men have been caricatured in the poem:

'Where the warfare is the hottest

In the battlefields of life,
You'll find the Christian soldier
Represented by his wife.'

Even if there are roles in church from which some people feel
women are disqualified on biblical grounds, this would never
excuse the attitudes which have led to the hypocrisy mentioned above and the generally demeaning attitude some
churches have towards women. Hence the need for the
change of mind and heart which is characteristic of repentance.

And this repentance should not only be 'corporate'. Many
women in our fellowships having been wounded by male-
dominated structures and attitudes. Where men are aware of
this, their simple but genuine personal apology to individual
women will do more to tear barriers down than any article,
book or sermon.

2 Break 'the patronising circle'

We must break 'the patronising circle'. Prejudice against
involving women in ministry often goes something like this:

1 'Women are not as good at public speaking as men.'
2 'I asked a woman to speak once and she wasn't very
   good.'
3 'This shows that women are not as good at public speaking as men!'

QED! Of course, the actual 'patronising circle' is argued in
a more sophisticated form, but the basic outline and end
result are much the same.

Almost all prejudice uses this kind of reasoning. But we
can break into it by approaching individuals on the basis of
gifting rather than *gender*. If women don't get many speaking
opportunities they are not likely to become good speakers.
But if we train, encourage and give opportunities to poor
speakers of both sexes (given a potential gifting in speaking)
we are likely to end up with some good men and women
speakers in our churches! And, of course, the same principle
applies to many other areas of church life.

3 Avoid tokenism

We must avoid 'tokenism'. It is superficially attractive to redress the balance in our congregations by making sure there is at least one woman on each committee or planning group. This has the advantage that it can be done fairly quickly. We must resist this option. Far from tearing down barriers it creates them. In principle, it treats women as inferior by insisting on a place for them by virtue of their gender, not on the basis of their gifting or calling. In practice, it breeds cynicism and resentment among men (and some women) and can lead to a new form of legalism in church life. But when churches are – quite rightly – put under pressure to address this issue, some have hurried down this cul-de-sac rather than taking the trouble to think it through properly.

4 Give positive encouragement

We must go out of our way to encourage women to develop their ministries. They are equal members of Christ's body who have not been (in general) expected or encouraged to have a significant contribution to make to the leadership of church life. This must change! Men in leadership must give the women in the churches a chance to say what they feel their gifts and abilities are and in what areas they feel they have a contribution to make, and then allow them to make it!

None of these ideas will reap rewards overnight but I believe that, taken together, they can begin the dismantling process which this wall of prejudice deserves.

The racial divide

God is in the business of reconciliation, by destroying the barriers that sin erects between himself and us. He has opened up the possibility of reconciliation not only with God but also with our fellow humans. Yet 2000 years after Paul declared that in Christ there is 'neither Jew nor Greek', racial and cultural divisions are still found within the church.

The revolutionary message of the New Testament is that God judges people on the basis of their relationship with

Christ, not on consideration of their culture, colour, political allegiance, nationality or race.

This must not remain in the realm of theory. As local churches we must demonstrate our commitment to these truths. It is easy enough to speak out strongly against racism in South Africa while practising a covert racism in our own churches and community.

There are many simple things we can do locally in this area without compromising the uniqueness of our faith one iota:

• Invite a converted Muslim or Hindu (or even an unconverted one!) to speak at your church. Much prejudice is based on ignorance. This will help by giving non-threatening information about the ethnic groups which share our towns and cities.

• Arrange a visit to a local mosque or synagogue. This will give significant insights in a very short space of time. Guaranteed to strengthen your prayer life!

• Encourage the church family to be on the look-out for those who stand alone at (for example) the school gates or in the works canteen – by virtue of their colour or race. Don't ignore them like everyone else!

• Interview representatives of local political parties in a church service. Pray for them.

• Put a managing director in the same home group as an unemployed shop assistant. Add a wealthy scrap metal dealer and an impoverished university lecturer. If you can get them to listen to each other and love each other, you will be doing a great deal to tear down walls established by class, intellect and social status.

Red and yellow, black and white ...

The different races may be precious in God's sight but that hasn't stopped people having an alternative view! Some of the mistrust and prejudice in our society has spilt over into the church. Christians in black-led congregations often feel that they have been misunderstood by white churches (if not deliberately excluded) and are nervous of links which could open up the possibility of rejection again.

Those in the 'white' churches must work hard to overcome the caricatures which bedevil these inter-church relationships. ('They never reply to my letters', 'they forget there is a meeting . . . or turn up an hour late!' etc.) Many black-led churches have pastors who are also trying to hold down a full time secular job, have little, if any, secretarial support and operate under different cultural constraints. (Do *we* have a divine mandate for our obsession with watches and diaries?!)

Ultimately, good links between churches of different racial or cultural backgrounds will depend on things like:

- Consistently working at it for many months, even years.
- *Personal* contact: dropping in at the house, having dinner together, watching a football match. All this beats a thousand letters and the odd phone call by a mile!
- Inviting their choir to sing at your church.
- Challenging them to a cricket match.
- Recognising that they often have more to teach us than we have to teach them.

In whatever situation our local church finds itself, much can be done to overcome barriers of these kinds. We must act with love, gentleness and patience. *But we must act*! Our growing health as a church in the next decade depends on it.

> 'Just as I am, Thy love unknown
> Has broken every barrier down;
> Now to be Thine, yea, Thine alone,
> O Lamb of God, I come.'
> *Charlotte Elliot*

2

Better Together

THE ISSUES

A group of clergy were gathered together for their monthly meeting. They represented all the denominations of the town and, to add a little variety to their normal proceedings, they decided to have a discussion about which denomination Jesus would join were he to return today.

The Baptist rose to his feet first. 'There's no doubt in my mind that if the Lord were to come back today, he would become an affiliated member of the Baptist Union. Baptism by full immersion is the biblical form, and he showed by his baptism in the Jordan by John that that is where his commitment would lie. A Baptist he would be.'

'Och, aye', the Scottish Presbyterian exclaimed as he rose to his feet. 'All things decently and in order, and *semper reformanda*. The Presbyterian form of church government, and predestinatory Calvinistic reformed doctrine would have the good Lord's hearty assent. A Presbyterian he would be.'

'Much as I would like to agree with you both,' interjected the Methodist, 'I would have to say that what our nation needs today is a holiness movement of the kind Wesley began, with open air preaching, and the hymns and the small group technique of his classes. A Methodist is surely what the Lord would become.'

One by one, the ministers, priests, pastors and leaders of the other denominations joined in the discussion with articulate, good-natured reasoning – the United Reformed Church, the Seventh Day Adventist, the New Testament Church of God, the Assemblies of God, the Pentecostal, the New Church, House Church, Roman Catholic, Brethren, until at last the local Anglican vicar rose to his feet and, with customary gentility, intoned: 'I say . . . really, I don't see what all the controversy is about. I don't see why our Lord, were he to return today, would wish to change his denominational allegiance to another church at all!'

Fragmentation and rivalry

The point is clear. The church, far from being 'all one body we' as the hymn puts it, is fragmented, splintered and divided by denominations and within its denominations. This is a scandal to the watching world, and undoubtedly grieves the Lord who prayed for the church he left to carry on his work: 'Holy Father, protect them by the power of your name . . . so that they may be one as we are one' (John 17:11).

Have you ever tried to nod your head and say 'no'? or shake your head and say 'yes'? It's almost impossible to do it without a huge effort of the will (although I have just discovered an Eastern European culture that does just that!). If we could manage it we would succeed in sending out two contradictory signals at the same time – and spread great confusion wherever we went! Yet the church has managed to perfect this amazing feat, affirming with a huge 'yes' that 'Christians are family' and 'we are one in the Spirit' while vigorously shaking its head, indicating the opposite by its disagreement, wrangles and divisions!

We must not fool ourselves into thinking this is merely an internal problem which we can 'hush up' by appearing at an annual ecumenical service or muttering darkly that 'it's the church invisible that matters'. The church *visible* is the only one non-Christians have any interest in! Richard Baxter felt the impact of this as far back as 1656:

'The public takes notice of all this [division] and not only derides us, but becomes hardened against all religion. When we try to persuade them, they see so many factions that they do not know which to join – and think it is

26

better not to join any of them. Thus thousands grow in contempt of all religion by our divisions.' (Richard Baxter, *The Reformed Pastor*. Edinburgh: The Banner of Truth, 1974.)

It seems that there are two options open to us as we relate – or fail to relate – to other Christians in this country. The first is to continue isolationist policies, as local churches and as denominations. Paradoxically, this option will simply weaken the local church further. The second is to learn to co-operate at all levels – between local churches, between denominations and between para-church organisations. It is this co-operation which will enrich, enliven and revitalise the local church. The 'Street Level' project in which Scripture Union has become involved, networks no fewer than thirty-six church congregations or Christian units, all within a one-mile radius of our offices. Working together makes so much more sense than the alternative duplication and competition for scarce resources.

Option one: disunity and weakness

One of England's evangelical leaders aptly describes that branch of the English church as 'the twelve tribes of evangelicalism' and one suspects that, year by year, the strands proliferate. Labels abound and, although they can be useful descriptive shorthand, more often than not they are the means of pigeonholing others into categories that clearly imply a 'them-us' relationship, and *they* are not one of *us*! Just think of some of those labels – evangelical, charismatic, pentecostal, reformed, protestant, catholic, liberal, anglo-catholic. Not to mention those applied to particular doctrines such as pre-, post- or a-millenialism!

Of course this is not to deny or undervalue the emphases behind the labels, nor the doctrines for which some of our spiritual ancestors went to the stake to preserve. But the biblical doctrine of the church is, as many of us say week by week in the creed, that of 'one holy, catholic and apostolic church'.

Factions and divisions are nothing new. The early church, often wrongly idealised by those who long wistfully for the purity of the New Testament church, also had its problems. If it hadn't, most of the New Testament letters would never have been written. Why else would Paul have written this to the church in Corinth:

'I appeal to you . . . in the name of our Lord Jesus Christ, that all of you agree with one another so that there may be no divisions among you and that you may be perfectly united in mind and thought . . . One of you says, "I follow Paul"; another, "I follow Apollos"; another, "I follow Cephas"; still another, "I follow Christ". Is Christ divided?' (1 Corinthians 1:10, 12–13).

The question demands a categorical 'No!' But the church in the last decade of the twentieth century is riddled with ever increasing divisions, seeming to pay little heed to Paul's vivid exhortation to the church in Corinth using the body as his illustration (1 Corinthians 12:12–31). It is true that Paul's main focus here is probably the local congregation, but the principles clearly apply on the broader scene as well.

Option two: co-operation and enrichment

Those who have had the opportunity of working in ministry in non-denominational or interdenominational circles, can see the advantages of co-operation. The mutual enrichment that comes from the whole, multifaceted body of Christ far outweighs the narrow-minded, possessive parochialism that can actually cause the local church to wither as it puts all its energies into its own activities.

There seems to be, at least in my experience, a discernible and direct correlation between an outward-looking missionary concern and the vital growth of a congregation's life. There are dangers here, and if chapter 12 of this book is misunderstood, there could be those who feel that so long as we give ten per cent of our income to missionary causes, God will automatically bless us with numerical growth, so solving our financial problems! There is more to it than that.

I remember the minister of one congregation, however, who forbade members of 'his' church to participate in any outside activities, particularly of an inter-church variety. His motives were unquestionably sound. He was concerned that the truth he was imparting to his people should not be polluted by teaching over which he had no control. But the end result was either frustration from church members who felt their adult choice was being restricted; or else a lack of awareness of alternative and complementary riches that could be found in the wider church. The life of that congregation eventually began to wither, as one after another quietly left for what they considered to be greener pastures. It need not have happened. The mutual enrichment that comes from the whole body of Christ, together with the sense of biblical discernment of mature and well taught believers, far outweigh the restrictive, inward-looking parochialism that some local churches seem to encourage.

On the English scene, phenomena such as Spring Harvest have contributed to a wider vision among a broad range of Christians. When over 80,000 gather together, about 10,000 over a week at various sites throughout the UK, something is bound to happen. And it has! To find so many Christians grappling seriously with the biblical implications of the occult, of humanism, secularism, the philosophy of writers such as Nietzche, and issues such as hermeneutics, the New Age, ecology and the like – makes an Australian mind boggle! It was a totally new experience for Marlene and me coming to England, to find such large numbers of evangelical Christians prepared to think biblically, and to work on such issues.

But, as with all good things, there are dangers here too and a balance is needed. We have never been in a country where so many Christian conferences are held! Some people seem to live 'on the circuit', going from one to the next, speaking, leading workshops or just attending. Some in the latter category are a bit like the 'groupies' who follow the stars in sport or pop music, only in this case their 'idols' are Bible teachers and workshop leaders. When such conferences are needed to give a periodic 'high', as if a 'fix' were needed to keep the spiritual batteries charged, there are danger signals for the life of the local church. As it is, many of the traditional church weekend houseparties have gone by the board, so that church groups go to one or other of the big conferences instead.

However, on the positive side of the balance sheet, all kinds of barriers between denominations have been broken down by this sort of event. Prejudices and preconceived ideas about Christians with other labels, from other denominations, or from other types of churchmanship, have been removed.

One of the issues raised by such events relates to what some call 'parachurch' organisations or movements. The *UK Christian Handbook* lists hundreds of such organisations. Some comprise only one or two people, others employ several hundred staff. All of them have come into being, ostensibly, to serve the church. Quaint phrases such as 'the handmaiden of the church' have come down from history as the ideal held by highly respected organisations which have served the kingdom well.

Literally, a 'parachurch' organisation is one which exists 'alongside' the church, making its resources and skills available so that 'the church' can fulfil its God-given task in communicating the good news to its contemporary generation.

The problem arises when such groups are perceived as

encroaching on the preserve of 'the church', whether that be understood as a denomination or a local presence. Theologically, as one who has spent a large proportion of his ministry in such organisations – firstly the Bible Society, and latterly Scripture Union – I would question how correct it is to use the term 'parachurch' at all. As with most labels, I find it unfortunate.

For example, Scripture Union has about 300 paid staff in England (over 1,000 worldwide) and many thousands of so-called 'volunteers'. Each individual (with some exceptions) is a fully paid up member of a local congregation, supportive of it, and often supported by it. Hence, we *are* 'church', all members of the body of Christ, which is the most apt biblical description. We are not 'the church', but we are certainly part of it, as much as all those others who faithfully attend their local church Sunday by Sunday.

We – and all other similar movements – dearly want to serve the wider church, with the skills and experience built up over many years that a local church (and often a denomination) is unable to muster. That is not arrogance; it's a fact.

But having also worked as a pastor for eleven years, I know the pressures faced by local ministers, for whom a 'parachurch' organisation is yet another pressure, asking to be put on missionary budgets, or to be able to preach on deputation, or to make some wonderful resource available! The solution is found in sensitive mutuality and humility. If we want to close our church in a decade, we will do it most easily if we feel we can minister to others all on our own, and that the richness of the wider church is a distraction or a nuisance, rather than a potential blessing.

It is unusual for a body that has so few practising members (at least in the UK) to be so newsworthy. Scarcely a day goes by without the national media making a story of public interest out of some church happening or other. In fact, this generation seems more than ever to be in a shopping mood for answers to the fundamental questions of life. The alternatives that have been offered and tried have only led to emptiness and disillusionment. The radicals of the 1960s and 1970s have become the conservatives of the 1990s. With such an opportunity confronting the church, it would be criminal if resources were not pooled. God's people need to work together, in obedience to Jesus' prayer that we might all be one, to reach this generation for him.

We do not need to be unified organisationally, clones of one another. Nor do we need some superchurch, with a superleader (apart from Jesus himself, of course!). But we do need to pull together and not apart, not compromising or sacrificing the truth, but acknowledging our non-essential differences. When we are serving one another in love (and allowing ourselves to be served, which is sometimes even more difficult), the 'one, holy, catholic and apostolic church' has a lot going for her. We may not understand why Jesus chose to propagate the faith through her as he has; I certainly don't. But let's acknowledge her potential beauty, attractiveness and strength – internationally, denominationally and in 'parachurch' movements – and be mutually enriched. How do we actually do that locally? Well, Steve has some good ideas!

THE WAY FORWARD

The first reason for improving relationships between Christians is a negative one – to avoid alienating the non-Christian world yet further! More positively, we are convinced that personal faith is developed, worship is enriched and evangelism is enhanced when our relationships are deepened with Christians involved in different structures and streams from our own.

Unity in the local church

The local church is filled with ordinary people who care deeply, pray faithfully and give generously. Sometimes these same people argue, gossip, backslide and fail. We haven't arrived but we are on a journey together to become like Jesus. So far, so normal! But some churches seem to have turned disunity into an art form – internal conflict is the rule rather then the exception. We must face this honestly. How can we expect the Methodists to get on with the Baptists when the Sunday School doesn't get on with the women's meeting in the same church?

Here are some practical steps we can take to promote unity within our fellowships:

● *Consult widely in the church family and develop a church plan.* Given some generally agreed objectives, different organisations can see where they fit into the overall plan and how they can most helpfully contribute to the life of that church. This breeds co-operation between various parts of the church, not competition.

● *Unity must be based on truth.* Godly confrontation can be the key to unity. Don't try to keep people 'at all costs'. Some differences may be irreconcilable this side of eternity. Remember that a loss to your church is not the same thing as a loss to the kingdom! 'Blessed subtractions' may be a step to unity.

● *Keep the focus of preaching, committees and church magazines positive.* People very quickly become problem centred and this can lead to a negative, downward spiral of discouragement, complaint and disunity.

● *Affirm all aspects of church life.* Some divisions in church life are caused by 'ergocentricity' – the 'my ministry is more important than yours' syndrome. Prayer ministry is not more valuable than social action – both are needed.

● *Remember that 'unity' is a fact!* We *are* united in Christ. Call the people to become what they already are in God. We are asking people to recognise their true position as Christians and to live in the light of what is a present reality; we are not seeking to impose a new set of principles by which the more 'spiritual' Christians ought to live. This apparently subtle distinction can have big consequences. There is a huge difference between telling a twenty year old to grow up and behave like an adult and saying the same thing to a fourteen year old. For the teenager it will require a herculean effort of will and understanding for him to comply; most likely he will simply give up the struggle. For the twenty year old the issue is entirely different – he already is an adult! We only want his behaviour to reflect that fact. This is the position the church finds itself in with regard to unity!

● *Remember that expressions of unity are a 'by-product'.* The more you preach about unity, talk about love and tolerance and criticise disunity, the more distant a united church appears. Unity (like fellowship) happens when our attention is focused *elsewhere*. Put a dozen men together in a room and tell them to 'have fellowship', and quite a few things will happen – but fellowship isn't likely to be one of them! Ask the same men to build a shed for a disabled pensioner, paint the church or plan an evangelistic dinner and, quite 'accidentally', fellowship results. Plan social events and task-oriented activities and unity will grow. When we have a divided house we must encourage action and activity with open arms at the front door; unity will slip in through the back!

Cooperation between local churches

Let's hear from Richard Baxter again:

> 'This we have seen to our sorrow. Instead of living with one another as one heart, one soul and one mouthpiece (to promote each other's faith, and holiness, and to admonish and help each other against sin), we have lived on the contrary in mutual jealousies, and drowned holy love in bitter contentions. We have studied how to disgrace and undermine one another to promote our party's cause. We have also drawn our people into these struggles, dividing and slandering one another.' (Richard Baxter, *The Reformed Pastor*, Edinburgh: The Banner of Truth, 1974.)

This may sound a bit extreme but, if we are honest, many local churches and leaders have thought and behaved in this way. In some of our towns and cities the best scenario is of an uneasy truce characterised by a sullen tolerance. Of course there are wonderful examples of situations where good relationships between churches exist and, happily, these appear to be on the increase. We can only rejoice when friction is reduced and godly tolerance and respect is increased.

How can we develop these relationships?

● *We can avoid being negative about other churches,* publicly and privately. This takes firm determination, especially at first. Far too often we relish the latest bit of negative gossip about another fellowship and delight in passing it on. Where we are confused by what we hear about another church, let's resolve to ignore the trivial and seek to clarify the important, face to face with the leaders of the church concerned. On almost every occasion I have done this, I have come away with a totally fresh perspective on the problem.

● *We can pray in our services for other local congregations.* Does a local church have a mission coming up? Is there one facing a change of minister? Is there a church that has planned some special services? These prayers open our congregation's eyes to the wider Christian family and are a real encouragement to the churches we pray for.

● *We can build personal relationships with other leaders.* As long as we can keep people at a distance it is easy to ridicule and criticise them. Take your courage in both hands and ring up that 'liberal' Anglican or that 'charismatic' Methodist – even if you are a 'boring' Baptist! Invite them round for coffee. Once you get to know people without their labels, genuine relationships become possible.

● *We can act together for mutual benefit.* Even if this is only to enjoy the 'economies of scale'. Smaller churches in particular could order similar literature, share a photocopier or pool resources such as videos, cassettes or books. Churches of all sizes could do a general audit of their plant, personnel and machinery. Almost every church will find that these are not being used to their maximum potential. In times of non-use, could they be shared?

Cooperation within denominations

Not only do local churches need to relate to each other but also to others in their denomination. Almost all churches, including new churches, have allegiances of this kind, although the scope of authority within particular denominations varies immensely. Some churches have legal and administrative relationships with their denomination's headquarters; others are almost entirely autonomous with merely a perfunctory acknowledgement of the denominational hierarchy.

In general, ties with denominational bodies are becoming looser as more churches seek relationships locally and nationally on the basis of theological position and ministry 'style', rather than denominational label. This 'de-denominationalism' has been evident for some time among ordinary Christians. When they move to a new community they are much more likely to look for a church which 'suits them' than one which happens to share the denominational label of their previous church.

As God continues to lead his people through the 1990s I suspect there will be a degree of unhealthy polarisation in attitudes to denominations. The extreme positions could be described as 'exclusive' arrogance on the one hand, and 'dismissive' arrogance on the other.

Partly as a backlash to the perceived drift away from the denominations, there are increasingly strident calls in some quarters for an aggressive denominational allegiance – if necessary at the cost of other relationships which transcend these denominational boundaries. On the other hand, it has become fashionable in some circles to dismiss the idea of 'denomination' altogether, ridiculing its structures as irrelevant at best, moribund at worst! It could, of course, be true that my denomination is better than yours *or* that my denominational structures make the dodo look healthy; but the attitudes which lie behind each of these positions can be potentially ungodly.

Surely local churches should express all the richness of the emphasis on the kingdom of God which the last twenty years have brought us. This kingdom is bigger than our denominations! Many of us have found a love for the risen Christ and an openness to his Spirit in Christians from an amazing assortment of churches – some we had written off years ago. Has God got no taste?! How could he bless people who are not as completely sound as I am?! And what about my own denomination? Behind those structures I so mercilessly expose are some godly men and women seeking to respond to God's call on their life. At the very least they deserve love and respect. And, who knows, perhaps they have chosen a harder, though ultimately more profitable task, than I have the stomach for!

Let's be known in the local church at least as much for who we are in favour of, as for whom we oppose!

Cooperation with parachurch organisations

Since the early 1960s parachurch organisations have become an increasingly significant factor in Christianity as a whole. The last two decades particularly have seen them grow explosively in numbers and influence. In fact, many of the exciting initiatives which have captured the imagination of thousands of Christians have originated from this source. Spring Harvest and March for Jesus (to name but two) were the products neither of a local church nor an historic denomination. They were both conceived by individuals operating in the context of organisations which are wider than any single local church yet not a traditional denominational grouping.

The local church and parachurch groups have not always had the happiest of relationships . . . and the suspicions continue! These tensions must be resolved because we need each other so badly. Local churches (and their leaders) have often been slow to respond to need, becoming more concerned with maintenance than with mission, suspicious of change and insecure. They have therefore become antagonistic to 'outside' interference. Parachurch organisations have often been patronising to church leaders, irresponsible in their evangelism and insensitive to local needs and priorities. Attitudes and actions need to change on both sides! But how?

• There needs to be a fresh recognition by both groups that we are on the same 'side'! We may have different priorities and be in different locations but we are working for the same kingdom.
• Parachurch organisations must *mean what they say* about being servants of the local church. They must listen carefully to it and not simply impose their own agenda on the church they are working with.
• Churches must *say what they mean*. What kind of mission

is required? What are the church's expectations of the para-church helpers? What end result is anticipated? All this must be clearly communicated.

• More pastors need to be willing to straddle both worlds. This is time consuming but is always to the mutual benefit of both parties. They need to give time to serve on boards or councils of reference, become prayer partners or encourage financial support from the church.

• Local church members should be increasingly involved in discussions about 'national strategies'. At the end of the day these simply will not work unless they are 'owned' and implemented at local level.

• Members of parachurch organisations must be responsible members of local churches – even when Sunday attendance is limited by the nature of their work.

• 'Conferences' should have a health warning on them. Too many can be bad for you! There are an increasing number of opportunities to be away from the local scene at camps, conferences, consultations, seminars and convocations. Many of these are excellent but going to *too* many of them can result in a critical attitude to the local church and become in itself a substitute for the more mundane, nitty gritty work of church life.

This decade of opportunity can be entered into with fresh confidence if we approach it together. It is within our grasp to achieve unity within local churches and co-operation between them, supported by all the resources of the wider Christian world, given and received with love and respect. As a whole church, we will most certainly be 'better together'!

'A new commandment I give unto you,
    that you love one another, as I have loved you;
    that you love one another, as I have loved you.
By this, shall all men know you are my disciples,
    if you have love for one another.'

Author unknown

3

Leadership

The church committee was in full swing. The preliminaries had been dealt with. The minutes of the last meeting had been adapted with the odd spelling mistake corrected, and pedantic alterations made to the grammar.

The discussion had become lively, developing into a heated debate on one particular issue. The chair held back, wanting there to be consensus, openness, non-directive leadership. For one and a half hours they argued, until at last he decided they had spent enough valuable time on this particular agenda item.

What could have been so important to have taken so much time? It was the length of the toilet chains in the church loos! Should they be long enough for children to use, or so short that only adults could activate them? In telling the story, the minister was making the point that uncoordinated group work such as a church committee can go nowhere fast, without leadership.

THE ISSUES

Leading meetings in a church, or any organisation, can be fraught experiences. My wife's ministry in lay training has an element of personality profiling, where she will work with a church leadership team, showing them how their natural personality differences are often the root cause of conflicts that so easily beset church meetings.

Once we understand what makes other people tick, much of the heat gives way to mutual understanding. Leadership then becomes a matter of drawing on the strengths represented in the group, while realising that unanimity, or even consensus, is not always possible. But agreeing to differ, and allowing the other view to be tried, releases the tension and enables progress to be made.

Does the minister always have to lead a meeting? Indeed, do meetings always have to have a leader? These are questions worth addressing, as we seek to mobilise the whole body of Christ. What does leadership mean in the context of the local church, and who should exercise it?

What sort of leader?

Many claim there is a crisis of leadership in the church today. In England, whenever the job of a bishop or archbishop is vacant, strident voices assert that the church's leadership is weak, resulting in flaccid compromise. One such leader was cruelly described as having 'firmly nailed his colours to the fence' on a particular controversial issue.

Magazines are published entitled simply, 'Leadership'. Books on the topic multiply, aiming to 'maximise leadership potential in the church' (See *Leadership Explosion*, Philip King, London: Hodder, 1987). Business and parachurch groups hold seminars and workshops throughout the country in an effort to strengthen leaders in their task. Secular management models are often used as the basis for such events, with 'pyramid', hierarchical structures given as the norm. The leader might be likened to a captain, coach or an orchestra conductor. One book lists a number of 'styles' of leadership; you can be the dictator, bureaucrat, counsellor, chieftain, patron, guru, executive, prophet, priest, king or elder. I'm sure the list could be extended, but it is exhausting enough as it is!

The fact is that, within the church, there are those who *want* to be led. They only feel secure when there is a strong leader giving directions and no questions are put their way. But not everyone fits that description; many others in our churches are being patronised, repressed or drastically under-used because of a leadership style that has no room for sharing or delegation, and sees no need for freeing up the gifts of God within the body of Christ.

One such person is a friend of ours. A doctor of medicine and an anthropologist, she has several years' missionary experience, both in the field and in an executive 'home' position. She was front person for a national television series bearing her own name, and had seemingly inexhaustible energies which she wanted to devote to the cause of the kingdom – and this included sharing mutually with her husband in the nurturing of their family. But in her local congregation, which they attended faithfully over a period of years, the *only* task she had been asked to do – and it was not for want of having made other offers – was to bake a plate of scones for a church function! Is it any wonder that there is a steady haemorrhage of competent church members, particularly women, when such an experience is not at all uncommon?

Sensible leadership demands the ability to discern or discover, nurture, train and liberate the gifts God has given to the local congregation.

Servant leadership

If anyone could have pulled off a 'one-man band' model of leadership, it was Jesus. But look at how he modelled leadership. At every point in his human life he chose another way. It was as if he set out to turn the secular models upside down.

Philippians 2 occasionally makes me choke up when I allow the full impact of the passage to strike home. Jesus didn't have to leave the love, security, comfort and glory of heaven with his Father, to come to this greedy, self-centred, cynical, rotten world. He didn't have to, but he did. And even as he did so, he could have chosen another way – not to be born in a humble stable, or to enter Jerusalem on a donkey for his final agony, or to die on a criminal's cross. But that is what he chose. Jesus,

'. . . being in very nature God,
    did not consider equality with God
    something to be grasped,
  but made himself nothing,

taking the very nature of a servant,
being made in human likeness.
And being found in appearance as a man,
he humbled himself
and became obedient to death –
even death on a cross!'

Philippians 2:6–8

As Paul wrote, to introduce that passage, our 'attitude should be the same as that of Christ Jesus'. A key to effective leadership, if Jesus is to be our model, is that of being a servant. 'Servant leadership' is written and preached about much these days. It is a style of leadership to which most Christian leaders would at least give their assent, but it is a style that is extraordinarily difficult to put into practice.

Society and the church both militate against such a style, with their tight, hierarchical structures. One bishop of the Church of England wrote that after he became a bishop, he always carried a towel in his pocket (it must have been quite a bulky pocketful!) to remind him of his servant status.

Not for Jesus the trappings of power, status, rank and glory. The symbols he chose to sum up his ministry were the towel, the crown of thorns, the donkey, the bread and the wine – all pregnant with meaning. They speak of humility and brokenness – the very antitheses of the proud positioning that is the mark of much of today's secular leadership and management.

It was just before the Passover feast, the very night that he knew he was to be betrayed. Jesus had modelled his leadership style for three years with his twelve hand-picked disciples. He had led them, trained them, encouraged and nurtured them, comforted and scolded them. He had lived with them, revealed his vulnerability to them – had given them himself, leading by example.

In a dramatic moment, he got up from the table and wrapped a towel around his waist. He poured water into a basin and began to wash his disciples' feet. They would have been bemused, confused, embarrassed. But he made it quite clear to them (and to us) what he was doing and why:

'I have set you an example that you should do as I have

done for you . . . Now that you know these things, you will be blessed if you do them' (John 13:15, 17).

Serving one another. Caring for each other. Mutuality. These appear to be the keynotes of Jesus' style of leadership, and he is the head of the church. How to put it into practice is the problem, when secular models of management – so often taken on board unquestioningly by the church precisely because they are secular – push for power and hierarchy.

Alan Martin, my predecessor as General Director of Scripture Union in England, once presented a paper on 'Leadership and Change' at a Chief Executive Officer's conference. In it he highlighted some of the tensions faced by Christian leaders who genuinely want to put Christ's principles in practice.

Directly related to what we have just been looking at, is the boss/servant tension. Alan's aim as leader was to 'create an environment in which staff could be firmly fulfilled and grow as Christians'. Such an aim would be equally desirable for a pastor or minister in a local church. But, whatever the situation, the tension remains. Can a pastor or leader consistently be a servant, while in a role where decision making and initiatives are expected?

I believe he or she can. Power has troubled me in recent years, particularly its abuse, and its use wrongly to repress others, whether in political or ecclesiastical terms. Then I came to realise that power was OK. The Bible contains many positive references to power and authority – of Jesus' teaching, of the Holy Spirit, of signs and wonders, to identify just three – but only on two counts: first, if it is not sought; and second, if it is used for the nurture, well-being and liberation of others. Within these two boundaries, it seems to me that power can sit comfortably on the shoulders of a servant leader. Otherwise power complicates, and the role becomes focal, which is why Jesus' role was not the source of his power or authority. As Messiah, he played havoc with the Jewish notion of one who would come in power to set them free. He came in weakness, vulnerability and humility, but with an inner power that issued from his relationship with his Father.

The servant leader

This inner security in a relationship with God the Father is the crux of the issue of leadership. Authoritarian, autocratic, directive styles are often directly linked with insecure, inadequate people, while consensual, participatory team leaders are able to empower others and delegate because they are secure in themselves, and have no need to prove their worth.

How well a pastor or minister is able to share leadership as a servant will depend on how integrated she or he is as a person. This relates to integrity, wholeness and shalom, modelling a genuine spirituality that the congregation can catch. There will be a consistency between the home and the church, so that a child of the manse won't have to say to a father (as I have heard it said): 'Dad, I wish you'd use your telephone voice with me sometimes!'

It will come from what I have begun to call, 'living life from the inside out'. There will be a disciplined commitment to working on the inner life, and not just preaching about it. It will be living and loving the Scriptures, and not taking them for granted, and communicating that love to a congregation both in preaching and lifestyle.

Richard Foster's, *Celebration of Discipline* and Gordon MacDonald's, *Ordering your Private World* are two contemporary classics that develop that theme. They ought to be read by anyone who wants to take servant leadership seriously. Congregations who have as their leaders people who are living a lie, are in a perilous predicament. Never has integrity in leadership been needed as much as it is today; and it has possibly never been such a scarce commodity, the spirit of our age being one of relativism, where no absolutes of right and wrong, good or bad, are tolerated. For the church to survive the decade, we need women and men whose walk with their God reflects their living relationship with Christ, attracting the world by the integrity, reality and beauty of that relationship.

When we were in Mauritius as young missionaries, my wife and I led a youth club. We had invited a Hindu Swami to talk to the club about Hinduism, so they could better understand that faith. At the end of the afternoon, I asked the Swami how he would define a Christian. After the briefest of pauses, and with much grace, he said: 'I would define a Christian as one who follows Jesus to the point of reflecting him.'

It's not the whole picture of course. But it's certainly not a bad litmus test of how our faith appears to others. The cliché that it is 'caught, not taught' is relevant not only for servant leaders, but for all of us who are followers of Christ.

THE WAY FORWARD

'I want to be a leader
When great success gives fame.
But I'm not so keen
With a failing scene;
And they're looking for someone to blame!'

When brickbats outnumber bouquets, the work never ends and you feel very much alone – who'd be a leader? Well, it's certainly not a role that should be undertaken lightly, not if we are expecting the approval of God and the respect of the people we lead. We ought to assess our personal life, our ministry style and philosophy, and how to reproduce these in others.

Personal life

The doctors' surgery my family are linked to offer an MOT (Men Over Thirty-five!) health check for those who feel well. It's based on the principle that prevention is better than cure. Church leaders, too, need regular personal check-ups to ensure that their spiritual health remains good. We ought to be asking ourselves some difficult questions – and facing up to the implications of the answers. Here are some of those questions:

Does my inner life reflect my public ministry?
One of the early warning signs of spiritual malaise is a growing divergence between what is said publicly and what is 'known' inwardly. Devotional times with the Lord become

perfunctory or non-existent, worship is increasingly formalised, evangelism an onerous duty and compassion a professional act rather than a burden of love. We need to be honest with ourselves here.

'Spiritual leaders do not pout. They may become vexed in their spirits, but they do not pout!'

Does my outer life reflect my public ministry?
Hypocrisy is an ever-present temptation for those who speak or lead publicly. While encouraging God's people to acts of commitment, sacrifice and devotion we can shy away from the cost of acting on our own advice. While heartily condemning the sins of the flesh we can be indulging in them. Sadly we can even hide behind the 'truth' that we ought to be proclaiming what is right, even if we fail to live up to it! Helmut Thielicke described this sort of hypocrisy as the process by which leaders build 'houses' of good works and godly living for the people they lead and then refuse to share the same accommodation.

No one can avoid hypocrisy entirely, but we must constantly be attempting to bring our words and actions into line with each other.

Is my life biblically 'balanced'?
There must be ingredients in my life which feed the whole person – body, mind and spirit. Without all three of these areas being addressed we are in danger of becoming 'unbalanced' as individuals. This will make us hard to relate to but also cause a good deal of inner tension. We have not been designed to work well on only one engine. It is possible, but usually leads to an 'unsteady' flight, shorter journey and unpredictable destination!

As the answers to these questions emerge we need some positive guidelines to help us get back to good health spiritually, and to stay there. Here are some suggestions:

• *Find a friend*! Or several friends – at any rate people you can trust completely. Give them the authority (and opportunity!) to probe your spiritual life. Isolation is one of the biggest causes of failure and burnout in ministry; we need trusted advisors who will encourage us, but who are not afraid to also confront and correct us. This is not always easy in the context of a local church and we may need to look outside the church for such help. Growing numbers of leaders are meeting in small 'clusters' with those from other churches for mutual help and correction in this way.
• *Build into your programme times for reflection*. Too often in local church life we are tyrannised by the urgent rather than motivated by the important. It is only in the periods of quiet reflection and assessment that we can clearly discern our priorities. These 'oases' of time can substantially reduce pressure and stress, keep us from going down a ministry cul-de-sac and help us 'tune in' to divine directions for ourselves and the church family.
• *Be human!* Take proper time for rest and recreation. Play with the children, make love with your spouse (if you're married!) . . . rent a video, sing in the shower, dip your biscuits in your coffee, go to see *Jungle Book*, listen to

Beethoven . . . whatever it takes – relax! Time with family and friends is an essential part of wholesome living.

• *Be healthy*. Many so-called 'spiritual' problems are rooted in the physical. If we looked after our bodies properly many of our other pressures would go. We need to cultivate good eating habits, times of exercise and adequate amounts of sleep. The most significant spiritual tonic for many leaders could be a week of early nights, a gentle jog round the block and a big bowl of muesli! The principle really is vital. Far too many church leaders today are caught up in a pressurised lifestyle and end up blaming God, the church, the demonic, and other leaders for the stress they feel, when in reality it is 'simply' the result of neglecting basic health care.

Ministry style

The first thing to note about ministry style is the power of example. We shout at the people of God in what we do and only whisper in what we say. That's why all the factors we have been looking at in the minister's personal life are so important. We must model something of the Christian life before people will follow us as we explain it and ask the church to respond to it.

Assuming our lives are characterised by integrity, what should our leadership style be like? Simply put, it should be like Jesus' style of ministry – servanthood. Ted Engstrom puts the position clearly when he says, 'Jesus is saying that leadership in its very essence is serving. It cannot be otherwise. To lead is to serve. And to serve is to become the servant of those one is leading.'

Obviously, this is partly demonstrated in our willingness to share the privileges and responsibilities of leadership (see Chapter 1) but it is seen even more fundamentally in our attitudes. How we need a revolution in this area! What a transformation our churches would undergo if they were led by leaders who were delighted with their function not obsessed with their status! We need leaders who steadfastly refuse to indulge in a leadership style which uses people and loves things; leaders who humbly recognise their dependence on God *and* the people of God, if true ministry is to be exercised and sustained. Mark Hatfield, an American senator, has some challenging words for us: 'We should be asking ourselves constantly: are power and leadership things I'm using to promote self, career and prestige? Or are they being used only as a way of serving Christ?' All of these attitudes lie at the heart of genuine servant leadership.

Before we consider the practical implications of servant leadership we must address a common misunderstanding. To be a servant leader does not mean a cringing, servile attitude nor does it imply a 'doormat' approach to leadership. Strong leadership and servant leadership are not opposites (see Chapter 5) – they can be complementary. We must always remember that we are servants of the church, but it is not our master – God is! The church should not treat me like a servant, but like a brother; God has the right to treat me like a servant – but he chooses to treat me like a son!

A servant-leader, then, is one who's life is characterised by *serving* not *servility*. His job is to do his master's bidding in all things and the result of this will be a happy master and a well-run household. Probably the most significant factor in a well-run church is the extent to which all the master's servants are functioning properly. The leaders may have been given a key role as 'head servant' but all the servants must play a part in serving the needs of the household. Far too many leaders think their servanthood means doing all the serving and far too many church members believe in letting them do it! An amazing number of people in our churches would readily own the title 'God's servant' but don't do any serving. Whoever heard of a servant who attended all weekly servant-briefings, was constantly reading the best-selling, '101 skills for a good servant' and who was always keen to develop these skills by going to conferences like 'servant harvest' . . . but who didn't do the job back in his own household, day by day?!

So the measure of success of a servant-leader is not just that he or she serves faithfully but also that he or she is leading the people of God into that same attitude and activity.

Leadership in the future

Not only must the church be well led in the present but

provision also needs to be made for it to be equally (if not better!) led in the future. This is a hugely neglected area in the Christian scene as a whole, but particularly in the local church. Provision must be made to identify, encourage, train and release those on whom the mantle of future leadership will fall. Failure to do this has resulted in countless churches having a period of life and growth which they have simply not be able to sustain. Key leaders have died, moved away or burnt out, and there has been no one to take their place. This is particularly true where churches or organisations have been built around a 'personality'. (Perhaps the true test of someone's leadership should be what things are like one year after they have gone!)

All leadership should have half an eye on the next generation of leaders. Who will they be? How can I help them develop? What experience can I give them? An investment of time and energy into this area will not be wasted. Indeed, Paul instructed Timothy to move on from being his apprentice and to start apprenticing others – who in their turn would instruct others, and so on (2 Timothy 2:2). Elijah had Elisha, Paul had Timothy; who do we have? Only a blinkered, short term view of progress in church life would ignore this future dimension of leadership.

Probably the greatest difficulty is in identifying who these future leaders might be. We are hindered by our memories – *we* were young and immature once and someone went out on a limb for us! We are hindered by our insecurities – what if they prove more able than we are? But most of all we are hindered by our prejudices. Given the numbers of leaders in the church who have been biased against women, young people, non-professionals and the poorly educated, it's a miracle that there is anybody at all in leadership, other than a few geriatric male professors!

I am always challenged by this recently 'discovered' application letter by the Apostle Paul to be a local pastor. Would you have employed him as your next leader?

'Understanding that your church is vacant, I should like to submit my application. I am generally considered to be an acceptable preacher, though I have occasionally been accused of lacking tact. I have also found time to do a little writing.

I am over fifty years of age and my health is not always good, though I still manage a full day's work making tents in addition to my many ministry activities. I have often spoken to large crowds in some of our major cities and have sometimes had to leave shortly after because of various riots and disturbances. I did not always get on well with the other religious leaders in the towns where I served and I have been threatened and attacked. I have also been in prison a few times.

I am occasionally forgetful, not being entirely certain, for example, who I have baptised! Still, God seems to have blessed my ministry and I believe I could bring some of this life to your church.

Yours faithfully,

Paul'

Not a promising leader by any standards! But how many Pauls have we missed out on because of our short-sightedness? May God deliver us from unbiblical presuppositions which blind us to the leadership potential of large segments of our congregations!

In summary, true leaders must be people of integrity, with the attitudes and actions of a servant, looking to release others into servant-leadership now, and in the future. Such leaders are worth following because they themselves are following Jesus.

> 'So let us learn how to serve,
> And in our lives enthrone Him,
> Each other's needs to prefer,
> For it is Christ we're serving.'

FROM HEAVEN YOU CAME
Graham Kendrick
Copyright © 1983 Thankyou Music, PO Box 75,
Eastbourne, East Sussex, BN23 6NW, UK
Used by permission

4

Administration: Getting it Done

THE ISSUES

It is said you can tell the sort of people who live in a home by the books on their bookshelves. There are those who would say you can tell the kind of manager that a pastor or minister is, by the amount of desk space that is visible!

It's not actually a fool-proof method. Sometimes I have been in studies where it is not only desk space that is the problem, but floor space as well, with books, magazines, and used visual aids looking as though a whirlwind had recently passed through. But in such vestries or studies, I have known the person in question, when looking for a particular cutting, article, book or resource, to home in on the right pile and find it without delay. Pity help the unsuspecting wife or husband who has the bright idea of tidying it up! Of such stuff are divorce statistics made!

'Structured' or 'laid back'?

Generally speaking, there are two types of people: those with neat and tidy minds, who like planning and do so in an ordered, structured way; and those who are commonly called 'laid back', who flow with the tide, perform spontaneously, and have been known to prepare sermons on the back of an envelope during a hymn before the sermon. (One such I knew became a bishop and was much loved for his preaching and pastoral skills!)

In every church, there will be a good mix of both types, each causing a good deal of frustration to the other. For the one, good administration and tidy structures are essential, while for the other, everything seems to turn out all right in the end, as they remain blithely unaware of the apoplexy and potential nervous disorders experienced by those on the receiving end.

For the church to function, some kind of structure and administration would seem to be wise. Having the hymns and readings chosen for services two years ahead may be going just a little too far, although I have known a minister who did so! But keeping everyone in suspense and putting people on the spot without warning can have unexpected consequences.

In one of our churches, I decided on the spur of the moment to ask an older member of the congregation to come out front and lead in intercessions. He was a saintly, godly soul, whose prayer life was an enrichment to me. Physically, he was in bad shape, crippled, asthmatic and with a weak heart.

A little flushed, and probably feeling he couldn't say 'no' to my request in front of 250 or so in the congregation, he came out and led in such a way that we felt the Lord was standing right alongside him, so real and alive were his prayers.

He struggled back to his pew, only to collapse with a heart attack. A doctor in the congregation went to be with him, while another member called the ambulance. As I began preaching, the ambulance men took him out on a stretcher. Passing in front of the pulpit, and looking up beatifically from the stretcher, he said so that all could hear: 'Don't worry about me. I can't lose either way.' He was sure of his ultimate destiny in heaven – as it happened, it was not to be then. But I have never forgotten that lack of planning is not always wise, fair or effective. He may have been a brilliant visual aid for my sermon, but it was grossly unfair on him, quite apart from the additional anxiety it caused the preacher!

'Professionalism' or 'led by the Spirit'?

One of the basic issues relating to structures and administration is the tension felt by some between 'professionalism' and 'being led by the Spirit'. As is so often the case, Christians tend to polarise, emphasising one to the exclusion of the other, an 'either-or' approach rather than the nearly always preferable approach of 'both-and'.

Why is administration somehow thought to be less spiritual than pastoral visiting, preaching or praying? When the gifts of the Spirit are referred to, more often than not the unusual, prophetic or supernatural ones are emphasised at the expense of the so-called 'natural' and 'ordinary' ones. But all are essential if the church is to survive and flourish. The Church secretary should be regarded (and treated) as being just as 'spiritual' as the house group leaders.

In 1 Corinthians 12: 28 and following, Paul lists the duties assigned to the various members of the body, all to be valued, and all 'appointed by God'. They are apostles, prophets, teachers, workers of miracles, those having gifts of healing, those able to help others (and surely that is all of us, so that none is excluded), *those with gifts of administration* and those speaking in different kinds of tongues.

Administration is to be highly valued. God intended things to be done 'decently and in order', although never to exclude the free movement of his Spirit breaking in unexpectedly, as he is wont to do! Not all will have the gift, and not all those who do have it will necessarily have *only* that gift. In fact, 'professional' administrators – those who do it for a living – may well need to be released into other kinds of ministry in their church life, so that church boards and Christian organisations become less loaded with accountants, lawyers and bank managers. In my experience, some of these latter make marvellous teachers, preachers, welcomers and pastors; while homemakers, teachers or the unemployed can be quite outstanding administrators.

The importance of planning and administration, and of having clearly defined functions, was made plain in the early church. It was growing rapidly, factions had developed between the Greek and Hebrew Christians, and the desperate needs of some widows were being overlooked (Acts 6). The disciples realised that 'the ministry of the word of God' was their priority, but that someone had to assume the important responsibility of distributing aid to the widows. So seven men were chosen, appointed and commissioned for the task. They were required to be 'full of the Spirit and wisdom'. No downgrading of administration here. On the contrary, there was a direct link between their appointment and the growth of the church: 'So the word of God spread. The number of disciples . . . increased rapidly.' And soon after, one of the seven, Stephen, 'a man full of God's grace and power, did great wonders and miraculous signs', and became the first martyr for the gospel.

Administration is honourable, and there is no fundamental dichotomy between Christian risk-taking and responsible management, between spontaneous spirituality and purposeful planning. We need to plan and think ahead, and we will look at that in more detail in the next chapter.

Spreading the load

Administration has a purpose, as do the structures that make it possible. It is to enable the job to be done, the job of setting free the people of God so that his good news may be effectively experienced by the world he loves so much. It is a question of spreading the load, which is what structures are meant to do. The problem is that so many structures actually reverse the process, so that a 'collar bar' becomes a bottleneck as the pastor or minister of the local congregation draws work to himself rather than devolves to others all that has to be done.

The story of Moses and Jethro is a good illustration of this (Exodus 18). Israel had been rescued from the Egyptians, and they made offerings and sacrifices to God in gratitude and praise for their liberation. Then Moses 'took his seat to serve as judge for the people, and they stood around him from morning to evening' (Exodus 18:13). When Jethro, Moses' father-in-law, came to visit him, he could see how heavy a burden Moses was bearing and asked him why he was doing it all on his own. Moses' answer clearly implied he did so because that's what the people expected him to do.

The pyramid model

Moses was wise enough to listen to his discerning father-in-law. His godly counsel was that Moses should choose capable men and make them leaders over thousands, hundreds, fifties and tens. Moses still dealt with the difficult cases, but the load was spread, authority devolved, responsibility delegated.

It seems a simple model. A pyramid would be the best diagram to describe it. But a pyramid with power at the top seems to run counter to what we have already seen of Christ's servant leadership, which surely must be our model.

Do we turn the pyramid upside down then, with the leader (in this case Moses) symbolically supporting or serving those to whom he has delegated the tasks? Have you ever tried balancing a pyramid upside down? And even if you could, propping it up to make sure it didn't collapse, what would the intense pressure per square inch be at the point where the apex of the pyramid touches the ground?

Either diagram falls down, it seems to me, when set alongside biblical principles. Either domineering autocracy becomes the model (top-down), or crushing pressure results (bottoms up), which may be why seminars on stress, and books or tapes on the topic are so popular among Christian workers these days.

The wheel model

There must be an alternative. One that could be proposed is the wheel. Taking Moses and his delegation of duties as our example (or Jesus with the three of his inner circle, then the twelve, then the seventy-two), it would be something like this:

● At the centre of the wheel is the *hub* (the pastor, minister or leadership team), holding it all together, but useless in isolation. It needs oiling and regular servicing.
● Coming from the hub, are the *spokes* (perhaps the house-group leaders), depending on the hub for their security, but incomplete and equally useless without:
● the *rim* (the office-bearers: the treasurer, church secretary, etc), which holds the spokes in place, and provides the base around which:

• the *inner tube* goes (those faithful Marthas and workers, cleaners and flower-arrangers, always there to do what needs to be done). Unseen, but essential, this provides the inflated pressure that then supports:

• the *tyre*: the congregation; the real ministers out there in the world, which is what the wheel is all about, where the rubber hits the road. It would not be effective without all the other components, but would be a limp and lifeless lump of rubber – which is what many of us feel like in the church if the whole is not working as it should!

So, once again we see that an interdependence and mutuality are integral to its structure if the church is to be effective. 1 Corinthians 12 is an appropriate passage here. We need each other. Structures are meant to enable the whole body of Christ to fulfil its God-appointed task, and not be a means of acquiring status, power, privilege or position. 'Why is it,' asks George Goyder, 'that the church today will not trust its members? Why does the church so often decline to recognise and to accept the activity of the Spirit among unregulated groups of Christians? Why is all initiative in the church expected and presumed to derive from the clergy? It is because we have substituted for the biblical doctrine of the Holy Spirit as ruler in the church a doctrine of our own, unknown to scripture: the authority of professionalism.' (The Peckles Church: A Layman's plea for partnership.)

The ministry belongs to the whole church, not just trained clergy (Ephesians 4:11–12, 25). The 'clergy-laity' distinction is not there in scripture, which talks of the *laos*, the people of God, all of us together. The words we use need to catch up with our theology here. We are all called to be ministers, and so long as the so-called 'laity' expect the so-called 'clergy' to be the professionals doing it all, and those expectations are taken on board, the church cannot be what God intended it to be. We need to encourage the devolution of tasks and a multiplicity of roles and functions. Many are there in scripture. This is the way to bring about freedom, mutuality and interdependence. How can it work? Over to Steve!

THE WAY FORWARD

Remember what it was like before you learnt to drive? It all looked so simple – after all, if your parents could manage it . . . ! Then came the day of your first drive: who had put 'kangaroo' petrol in the car? How could you be expected to change gear, look in the mirror and indicate at the same time?! What seemed so simple in *theory* left you exhausted, bemused and discouraged in *practice*. Perhaps the bus was better after all!

I don't know a church leader who hasn't experienced something of this in church life. Perhaps you're a keen young leader straight out of Bible College, bursting with ideas to try out on an unsuspecting congregation. Perhaps you're an elder, deacon or house group leader who has just attended a marvellous, life-changing conference and now you want to convince the rest of your church about it. Or maybe your ministry has been through a bad patch and you think the church can be revitalised by putting into effect some of the principles you've just come across in an exciting new book! All of us are faced with the task of turning theory into practice; putting excellent ideas into effect so that they *work* as well as sound good.

We need to think through *exactly how* we will develop these better administrative structures and that effective spread of work load, in our churches. Otherwise we'll end up with the same frustration that our learner driver feels, only magnified a hundred times over! Good men and women have been broken in their ministry because of this gap between theory and practice. High ideals, biblical plans and godly desires have been shattered in pieces in the storms of congregational life. It is not an exaggeration to say that in the turbulent waters between theory and practice, many a ministry has been shipwrecked. In the process, many a leader sinks without trace and many a church is left rudderless and damaged.

How do we move from the existing situation – a top-heavy one where a stressed 'élite' run themselves into the ground while the rest of God's people are denied a full role in his work – to one where everyone is fully and satisfyingly employed?

Decision making

The first thing that needs to happen before any change takes place is a decision! The church and the leaders need to be convinced that the present structures and organisation should change; and should then take a decision to change them! Without such a positive and definite decision, nothing gets done.

But exactly *what* should be done? How can we home in on what changes are needed? Here are three factors:

● *Be open to God.* Jesus really is the head of the church. What he wants, he is supposed to get. Usually, we just nod in his general direction to get a blessing on our own plans. He must be actively consulted!

● *Be open to the people of God.* We must listen carefully to members of God's family – even the ones we don't like. Their moans, ideas, insights and dreams can all have something of God in them.

'So the vote is as follows: Larry, Ruth, Dan, Sid, and Marcia are for the proposal. God and I are against.'

● *Be open to the other leaders.* Prayer and consultation are not substitutes for the church leaders giving their time, thought and energy to the matter. The people of God will need to be guided (but not bullied!) as decisions are made.

In practice (and depending on the importance of the decision), this will mean calling the church to prayer and possibly to fasting ('open to God'). They will need to have the opportunity to comment and make suggestions, before a small group, often the leaders, prepares a discussion paper outlining alternatives ('open to the church leaders'). This needs to be presented to the congregation for consideration – the format will depend on congregation size – and time given for reflection, prayer and feed-back ('open to the people of God'). After this, a decision can be taken. Different churches will have different 'mechanisms' for taking it.

There will of course be other ways of doing this, but it is important to make sure that the three 'open to . . .' principles are taken fully into account in the process chosen.

Structures

Making good decisions in a church with bad structures is like driving with the handbrake on! Progress is slow. With the right structures in place it is possible for the effect of good decisions to be felt much more quickly.

Many churches are so busy *doing* that they have no time for *assessing* whether they are doing things in the most effective way. It would be an extremely productive exercise in most churches to ask these six questions of its structures – that is, of every meeting, organization and activity:

1 What was its original purpose?
2 What is its aim now?
3 Is it accomplishing its aims?
4 If so, how? If not, why not?
5 Could anything else accomplish these aims more effectively?
6 What are your dreams for this organization at its best?

The congregation will find this exercise far less threatening if you make sure that:

- You give a clear explanation as to why it is being done.
- They understand that *everything* (including the leadership structure!) is being examined.
- You involve them in analysing their own areas of work.
- In the report-back stage you are as positive as possible.
- You discuss the *programme* not *personalities*.

For the majority of us this structural examination is long overdue. Careful implementation will bring significant results.

Jesus was quite certain that the religious structures of his day would have to change in order to accommodate the in-breaking of the kingdom. If they didn't they would tear apart under the strain, like old wineskins with new wine in them. The last twenty years have seen a surge of spiritual activity. God has graciously brought all sorts of gifts and ministries into church life – hardly a Christian fellowship has not felt something of its impact. Signs of life abound. Sometimes it's messy, confusing or even annoying but God is certainly at work! Our structures must adapt to this fresh life or it will spill out into other structures which can contain it and harness its life.

And our structures must change for another reason – because our society is changing! I suspect that the vast majority of our congregations have no idea how dominated the church is by the culture of the past. The times of our services have more to do with milking time than a biblical directive. And what about those who insist that the morning is the most appropriate time for the Lord's *Supper* or that the organ is the divinely appointed instrument of worship (it was actually banned in 1644 by Oliver Cromwell). And the list could go on. Of course, none of these things should be changed simply because they reflect the past. But we must hold to these things more 'loosely' – ready to change them if they get in the way of the task God has given us to do. This is a crucial point. Lots of churches are more committed in practice to the inerrancy and infallibility of their structures than they are to the mandate of God's unchanging word!

Our structures must be servants and not masters in the church. They must be flexible enough to cope with a changing world *and* fresh direction from a living God.

The gift of administration

So we are driving along, with the hand-brake off, enjoying the open road. But it won't last! Our car will need fuel, checks on tyres and oil, and regular servicing. This is what administration does for the church – keeps it going.

In some circles administration is belittled as an invasion of the secular into the spiritual; the implication being that it is a poor substitute for the work of the Spirit. I have had this argument explained to me in such forms as, 'Jesus didn't need a photo-copier so why does the church'(!) all the way to 'if this (activity) is of God, he'll make sure it happens. He doesn't need our help!' Now, of course, we must never replace dependence on God merely with efficient administration. But these two things are friends not enemies. Administration is a *spiritual* gift. God has given it to the church to enable his plans to get off the drawing board into a life-size working model. We must recognise the value of this gift, try to identify those who have it, then encourage and train them and put them to work. Despite appearances to the contrary a disorganised, inefficient church does not honour God.

And there is so much for good administrators to get their teeth into, extending and helping other ministries already in operation. For example:

● *Pastoral care*: letters can be written to people on their birthdays or special anniversaries, pastoral visits can be co-ordinated, leaflets on key issues (debt, child benefit, bereavement, etc.) can be ordered and made available.
● *Leadership*: appointments can be made on behalf of leaders, diaries planned, lists updated, resources gathered, sermon illustrations collated, information passed on. What a huge release this is for a busy leader!
● *Evangelism*: local information can be discovered, surveys undertaken, a wide range of literature reviewed, publicity overseen, links made with local media, phones staffed, and venues booked.

Social action, Christian education – the list just goes on and on. Good administrators can have a significant impact on all other ministry areas.

This spiritual gift can not only profoundly affect our ability to 'get the job done'; in doing so it can raise the level of respect in which the church is held, both by the community and by the non-Christian organisations to which it relates.

Two problems of the 1990s

Before moving on from this chapter we should pause for a moment to consider two dilemmas which face the church in a particularly stark way in the 1990s. These issues impact local congregations in a way which is unique to this generation, and they show signs of increasing in the next.

Information explosion

No wonder churches and leaders are confused about what their priorities ought to be; never before have we been engulfed by such a tidal wave of books, magazines, videos, cassettes and conferences! And not just from our own culture. We are now exposed to 'how they do it' in California, South Korea and Brazil. The sheer volume of this material, combined with its diversity – culturally, theologically and denominationally – makes the head spin. Now, as never before, the gift of discernment is desperately needed in our churches. 'All these things may be good, but which of them does God want *us* to concentrate on *now*?' This is a question which ought to occupy our prayer and leaders' meeting agendas.

Church 'fashions'

Various theological matters have surfaced at different points in church history as being the critical issues of the day. But these have often been doctrinal issues rather than specifically matters of church practice and were usually significant for a number of decades. Today there is an increasing tendency towards 'fashions' in church issues. One practical subject will surface and capture everyone's attention, only to be followed eighteen months later by another. In the last twenty years we have seen Leadership, Worship, Social Action, Signs and Wonders, Prayer and Prophecy (to name but a few!) fêted as the most significant thing to be 'into'. The effect on local churches and their leaders is like being on a roller coaster on which the brakes have failed. No sooner have we recovered from the shock of being told that 'God is on the side of the poor' than we are catapulted to the dizzy heights of expecting a miracle whenever we meet. We have barely caught our breath before we are flung round a tight corner into experimenting with the prophetic and turned upside down in discovering that none of it will work without a prayer concert! Churches everywhere are reeling from the effects of this 'ride'.

Now *all* of these issues are important; very important. I thank God that they have been re-emphasised in church life. But something is unhealthy in the way they are presented, when prayer (for example) can be dismissed as 'yesterday's agenda'! Many churches have no sooner started to put something into practice than the 'something' changes. We are in grave danger of producing Christians who have tasted everything and swallowed nothing; aware of all the significant issues, especially the latest ones, and yet dying of malnutrition through lack of feeding on a staple diet. These changing 'fashions' can cause us to mistake activity for progress. We can become 'merry-go-round' churches, characterised by lots of bright lights and music but going round in circles!

We need congregations and national movements which will see issues through to the point where they are rooted thoroughly in hearts, minds and wills. God may well want different emphases in different communities and church groups. Of course, we must always be open to changes of direction and always ready to affirm the full breadth of what the Bible teaches. However, in deciding what God would have us do at any particular point in the life of our congregation, we must have depth as well as breadth.

The next decade deserves a church which makes wise and godly decisions about what its priorities should be; and which implements these decisions in the context of flexible structures, efficiently and spiritually administered.

> 'O breath of life, come sweeping through us,
> Revive Thy church with life and power.
> O breath of life, come, cleanse, renew us,
> And fit Thy church to meet this hour.'
> *Elizabeth Porterhead*

5

Going for Growth

THE ISSUES

'He took his church from 175 to 12,000 in fifteen years. It's phenomenal!'

'Founded in 1980 with thirteen people, this church now has a membership of 5000 with two other 2000-member churches planted out.'

Both these statements, one spoken, the other written, have been communicated to me today, and such stories are the delight of the Christian press. The bigger the better, it would appear, and whether the local church is in an idyllic rural setting or a deprived urban one, to 'go for growth' seems to be the order of the day.

The sense of guilt and failure becomes enormous with the constancy of the message. If it weren't bad enough to hear all the success stories locally, it becomes worse to hear of how God is blessing the church in places like Korea where thousands meet in the early hours of the morning for prayer, and thousands more fill numbers of Sunday services, and all in one church!

In Africa, the statisticians tell us, the onward tide of Islam has been reversed and the continent will be predominantly Christian by the year 2000. Some bishops have confirmation services with candidates numbering in the hundreds, so rapid is the growth, while the general picture in England is of a declining established church where many local congregations have not seen any confirmations for years.

Indeed, with less than ten percent of the general population of this country going to church at all, going for growth has become a wistful hope for most.

I can identify with the feeling. Having moved from a job in Africa with the whole of the continent as my 'patch', travelling to forty-two of the fifty-one countries there, coordinating a staff of over 300, and with a sizeable budget, it was not easy to adapt to a local church with a main morning congregation of twenty-three! And yet I learnt an important lesson. Within a few short weeks, I discovered I was having contact at depth with more people, and with more purpose, than in the years of glamorous evangelical jet-setting. I realised that God is not only in the thunder, earthquake or mighty wind, but also in the still small voice. Small can be beautiful. Big congregations can present real problems — superficiality and impersonality being just two.

Planning

The problem all too often is that growth, when it comes, is unplanned. Like Topsy, it just happens, and the structures are unable to cope because goals and strategies don't exist. On the other hand, there are those who spend so much time talking about goals and strategies, reading books about them and attending seminars on them, that the task doesn't get done.

A group of priests went to a monastery for a weekend retreat. It was Friday evening, and they all joined together for compline, a service of prayers at the end of the day. There were four different orders represented at the retreat: Dominicans, Benedictines, Franciscans and Jesuits. Soon after the service began, the lights went out and pitch darkness enveloped the monastery. The Domincans prayed on, oblivious to the darkness, as they knew the service off by heart. The Benedictines fell to their knees and prayed fervently that light might be restored to the monastery, so that they could follow their service book and continue with compline. The Franciscans sat back in their pews and launched into a profound philosophical and theological discussion as to the relative virtues of darkness and light. The Jesuits got up, went out, and fixed the fuse.

Churches can be a bit like that. There are those who go through the routine of church life; others who pray for growth but do nothing about it; others who theorise about it all; then there are also those who know what needs doing and do it – the fuse fixers.

Context

In terms of goals and strategies going for growth can become a dynamic way of life. The first step of the process is understanding the *context* of ministry. For a local congregation, it will mean an awareness of the local community, its history, customs and culture. It is not uncommon for enthusiastic, recently-arrived pastors to catch foot and mouth disease as they begin their ministry, eager to turn their world upside down: they open their mouth and put their foot in it, unaware of their insensitivity.

I well remember when we wanted to put banners at the front of the church. There were war memorial flags hanging out from the side walls obscuring the places where the banners would go. So I suggested that we move the flags to the back of the church, and place them (appropriately, I thought) over the war memorial boards there. Wanting the support of the congregation, I warned them of my plans. It was as if a Third World War was about to break out, so strong was the opposition! It is, perhaps, a trivial example, but I had been insensitive to the church's history and context. But it did not prevent me from moving the flags, late one night and with the help of a cooperative church warden, back one pillar, leaving the banners clearly visible. No one even noticed!

The target audience

Then there is the *target*. Who are we aiming to reach? 'If we aim at nothing, we are sure to hit it.' It can be surprising to discover a wide variety of target audiences in any local church, each perhaps needing a different strategy to bring them into the life of the church. It might be young street kids, single parents, businessmen, staff of the local hospital, teachers at the local school; the list is almost endless. Growth, whether it be quantitative or qualitative, will not be likely to happen without the necessary homework and planning being done.

Resources

Once the target has been identified there needs to be a realistic assessment of the *resources* available to do the task. It would be no use, for example, aiming to reach the 750 children of the local housing estate, planning to have a holiday club, and starting up a Sunday School for 250 of them, with only two octogenarians and a sixteen year old to do all the work! Realism is a great ally in setting goals and devising strategies, so long as it does not become a means of hindering the Spirit.

Expectations

With adequate resources, we can go on to determine realistic *expectations*, and these will need to be broken down into measurable components. How many are likely to be able to be visited, for example, and are likely to respond? How many groups could be set up? How many leaders trained? But expectations are not only numerical. There are intangibles, too, wherever people and God are involved. How does one measure forgiveness, reconciliation, repentance, new beginnings? Statistics must never be allowed to stifle the unexpected work of the Spirit, but nor should spiritual spontaneity be an excuse for lack of strategic thinking and planning.

A danger

If we are going to take goal setting and strategic planning seriously, we need to beware of the danger of jargon. It abounds, and can be a camouflage for lack of action. The books, videos, tapes and seminars on growth are full of technical jargon and we need to be careful that we don't simply spout this to our unsuspecting congregations. They can quickly be put off any idea of growth simply from being barraged with a whole arsenal of unfamiliar terms.

We should not go to the other extreme though, and deduce that the process of strategic planning and goal setting should be avoided because none of the terms used in the professional literature are biblical ones! On the contrary, the concept of goal setting is a thoroughly biblical one. Let's look at some examples.

Biblical strategists

In Luke 12:25–35 we find Jesus surrounded by the crowds. Most of us would have been tempted to capitalise on their enthusiasm and curiosity by preaching a cheap gospel with few demands. Not so with Jesus. He did not mince his words in confronting the crowds with the true cost of being one of his real disciples. He used striking Hebrew phrases, like 'hating' even parents and family (meaning putting God first, even before such close family ties), and 'carrying the cross'. And he spoke about counting the cost, like someone planning on building a tower, or a king preparing for war.

In each case, goals and strategies are involved. The person who builds a tower or goes to war, has a clearly defined goal and carefully thought-out strategies. He needs to know that there are adequate resources available if the exercise is to succeed. 'Will he not first sit down and estimate the cost?' And, 'Will he not first sit down and consider whether he is able?' These two questions clearly indicate that Jesus thought goal setting and strategic thinking were vital in the Christian life. They are essential for us to succeed.

Another of many possible biblical examples is Paul, perhaps the greatest missionary and church planter the world has seen. He described himself as 'an expert builder' (1 Corinthians 3:10). In the same passage he pinpoints two essentials to growth in the church when he wrote: 'I planted the seed, Apollos watered it, but God made it grow' (1 Corinthians 3:6). On the one hand, there is the human involvement, but on the other, only God could give the growth, not working in divine independence, but using and blessing the efforts of Paul and Apollos. The record of Paul's missionary journeys are a testimony to the value of strategic thinking and planning. It was as if he had asked himself how, with the limited resources he had at his disposal, and with the restrictions of time and distance, he could establish the gospel throughout the then-known world. He chose the strategic centres of influence, right up to the household of the emperor in Rome, and planted the seed there. If he could plan on a *global* scale, how much more should we be able to do so in a *local* setting?

Then there was Nehemiah. His goal was clear. It was to

rebuild the crumbling walls of Jerusalem – against all odds, as it happened. He prepared for this gigantic task by praying and fasting. That was part of his strategy, not just a routine act, like 'opening with a word of prayer' before a Christian activity:

> 'When I heard these things, I sat down and wept. For some days I mourned and fasted and prayed before the God of heaven' (Nehemiah 1:4).

But Nehemiah wasn't like the Benedictines in the story, as they prayed fervently for light to be restored to the monastery. He backed up his prayer with action, going up the valley by night to examine the wall (2:15). He needed to know where the problems and opportunities were, and so do we if we don't want to see the church metaphorically in ruins by the end of the decade.

Furthermore, Nehemiah knew full well he was not going to be able to do the job on his own. Rebuilding the wall was not the task for a one-man band, nor is building up the church. What a motley bunch of 'builders' they were, from all different social classes – 'Jews ... priests ... nobles ... officials' and 'others' (2:16) – from different families and various locations, all with special tasks and all highly organised! Chapter 3 of Nehemiah makes fascinating reading, giving the impression of a busy army of ants all at work on a mighty task, oblivious to the ridicule and opposition they faced.

The fixing of gates, bolts, bars, beams, doors; the repairing and restoration of walls, towers and roofing; the work being done by goldsmiths, merchants, rulers of districts, residents of various places, fathers, sons – what a hive of activity it was! The people were motivated. When Nehemiah presented them with the picture of the broken down city, and the vision of what it *could* be like, they responded, 'Let us start rebuilding' (Nehemiah 2:18), and 'the people worked with all their heart' (4:6).

There was a clear goal and strategy, there was planning and organisation, there was cooperation. The people were motivated because their skills were being used and they knew what they were aiming for. There was a sense of shared responsibility; Nehemiah's authority was delegated, although he held it all together. There was a sense of common purpose in spite of difficulties, the odds stacked against them and the angry opposition of Sanballat. They all 'owned' the task. And finally, the task was done. The goals were met. The strategy was successful. And these methods are still biblical!

As we face the enormous task of surviving and growing in this generation, our churches need to hear and heed Nehemiah's call to action:

> 'The work is extensive and spread out, and we are widely separated from each other along the wall. Wherever you hear the sound of the trumpet, join us there. Our God will fight for us!' (Nehemiah 4: 19.)

We need to pray not for tasks equal to our powers, but for power equal to our tasks. Nehemiah and his co-workers found their powers to be adequate. May we find it so, too.

THE WAY FORWARD

Whatever happened to Church Growth? In the 1970s and early 1980s it was hard to walk around the Christian scene without tripping up over a Church Growth conference or consultation. Dozens of books identified skills, techniques and principles about how to increase the size of our churches. Countless other books and magazines outlined actual case histories where rapid growth had been experienced. In the last few years, however, this stream of literature has slowed to a trickle. Why is this?

Critics point to an over-dependence on American material, a problem with certain aspects of the teaching (eg the homogenous unit principle – that churches grow best when composed of similar people), an absence of community and social emphasis and a perceived dependence on technique rather than God's Spirit. All these criticisms have some foundation, and obviously we would be foolish to ignore the challenge they present. However, a more significant reason for the demise of interest in church growth could be related to the serious challenges it posed the church, the radical nature of its remedies and our unwillingness to pay the price of implementing them.

Despite the dangers (and they are real), numerical growth must be moved up the priority list of the local church. God wants people to get to know him – and then go on growing while they help other people to meet him. If God's will is to get done there will have to be lots of big churches and/or lots and lots of small churches to get them all in! There are, of course, specific individual situations where the church will not grow numerically; but this must not soften the impact of the inescapable logic of New Testament teaching and practice: it is God's 'norm' for the church to grow.

And the initiative for this growth must come from the local church leadership. Of course, grass-roots opinion can trigger action among the leaders; but at the end of the day relatively little is likely to happen unless the leaders are genuinely committed to it. All the studies of growing churches, both in the UK and overseas, point to the crucial role of the pastor or other leaders in stimulating growth in the churches. Or, to put it negatively, in the thrombosis of the church the minister is often the clot! He is the one usually causing the church's decline, or allowing it to do no more than simply 'hold its own'.

Leadership that leads to growth

As I have travelled and talked with leaders in growing churches I have discovered that three characteristics of their leadership seem particularly to contribute to growth.

Vision

AW Tozer has reminded us that 'the difference between the priest who has read and the prophet who has seen is as wide as the sea'. We must be leaders with a prophetic vision. Brilliant administrative gifts, a sound theological education and a multitude of clever ideas cannot make up for a lack of vision. The urgent task of the leader who has a desire to see church growth must first be to see God and get his vision for the church. Armed with this vision, we can go on to explore the specific needs of our own locality to arrive at an 'earthed vision', that is, God's mandate specifically applied to our situation.

Far too many of us as leaders have become so immersed in the work of the Lord that we have neglected the Lord of the work. Our leadership may be efficient, but it is often totally devoid of the divine presence. The fire of God remains in the heavens while the offering of our daily work remains sodden in the waters of routine and powerlessness (cf 1 Kings 18:20–39).

Our urgent task is to seek this fire from God, and not as some once-in-a-life-time experience but as a habit-of-a-life-time experience. Practically, I believe this means giving priority time to the devotional life, putting in the diary periods of fasting, and setting aside time to examine all aspects of our personal and church life in God's presence.

Despite its vital importance, this is only one aspect of receiving vision. For many leaders their ignorance of God is exceeded only by their ignorance of the world! We must give time and attention to finding out what is really going on with people, their deep concerns and their most pressing problems. What a sad sight so much of the church is, giving solutions to dilemmas few can relate to and offering answers to questions no one is asking! We need to address ourselves to the real issues facing an increasingly sophisticated, depersonalised society rushing towards the end of the twentieth century. We must hear from God if we are to be part of his mission to the world; we must hear from the world if we are to be a relevant, powerful part of the same mission. Both aspects are required for an 'earthed vision'.

Leaders who lead
This second aspect seems so obvious that I hesitate to mention it. In practice, good examples of leaders who lead are in short supply. Leaders must lead, elders must be allowed to 'eld' and deacons to 'deac'!

Invariably, a growing church has leaders who are not afraid to make unpopular decisions, suggest major changes or take risks. They are usually enthusiasts and always hard workers. Churches with an unhealthy emphasis on democracy or an unwieldy committee structure tend not to grow. The point at issue here is, do they actually *lead* or is the main role of leadership in our churches a *reactive* one? Responding to pastoral crises, congregational pressure groups and fabric needs is important but what about our pro-active role? Shouldn't godly leadership be having a positive input into the life of the body? Examine a few of the agendas of your leaders' meetings. How much material is there because of pressure from God and how much because of pressure from members? Growing churches need at least as much pro-active material on their agendas as reactive.

Setting goals

Leaders in growing churches know where they are going. This may not be expressed in numerical terms – £100 a week more in the offering, twenty-five new members this year – but clear direction is established, and even some short term destinations.

Real change will require us to be ruthlessly objective. Why are we doing this? What is it accomplishing? Can it be done better? Should we be doing something else? Don't be fobbed off with 'we've always done it', 'people are blessed (oh dreaded cliché!) by it' or 'you mustn't upset those who attend'. Yes, all this may be true, but are people being converted or discipled? Is worship improving? It is so easy for churches to drift for years without accomplishing anything significant.

I take as read, of course, that the *Holy Spirit* makes churches grow; the above paragraphs simply identify the kinds of leadership he often seems to use! But how does this visionary, pro-active, goal-setting leadership go about involving the church family in this exciting adventure?

Motivating the church

Many excellent books have been written about motivating a church to grow; some are recommended in the list of resources. What follows comes from my personal struggles in this area and the struggles of others that I have observed.

Defeating fear

● *Fear of growth.* It is safe to assume that when many people say they want the church to grow, they don't mean it! Lurking behind a superficial agreement with the 'idea' of growth lies a range of anxieties, often unexpressed. 'Will I be able to sit in the same seat? . . . Park near the church? . . . Still talk to the pastor?' 'Will it still be "my" church?' 'Will the new people change things?' 'Won't it all become big and impersonal?' People must be encouraged to express these fears and they need to be addressed sympathetically, but firmly. Lots of congregations give a unanimous vote for growth, and then leaders can't understand why people seem to be dragging their feet. Hidden fears are often the problem.

'I tried to tell him not to change the order of service.'

● *Fear of failure.* Lots of folk feel battered about by the storms of life; they may sing about having an anchor which is 'steadfast and sure' but they don't always feel it. And what if this church growth 'thing' fails? They will feel even more like failures – but with the added dimension that their church is a failure too! 'Shouldn't we leave well enough alone?'

The leaders must make a clear statement that pastoral needs will not be neglected. Sermons, Bible studies and prayer times should emphasise the greatness of God, and his ability to work with only a little faith. This fear must be tackled with patience and perseverance. The most negative, fearful fellowships can be changed!

● *Fear of 'unspirituality'.* King David counting his army (2 Samuel 24:1–10) has a lot to answer for! For some reason this story has been used by some Christians as an argument against any assessment of resources. Add to this a general mistrust of 'business' methods and we can see why all the analysis which church growth demands, is viewed with fear.

Isn't it just the *wisdom* of man trying to do the *work* of God?

The church family must be encouraged to see that analytical tools are not a substitute for dependence on God nor an enemy of it. Most Christians think carefully about things like their family budget, the children's education and provision for their parents – the Christian family deserves no less!

Developing goals

It's great to be part of a team which scores goals. Far too many churches have paid so much attention to training, the state of the 'pitch', having the right kit and practising the lap of honour, that they have forgotten the point of the game – to score! We are supposed to be accomplishing something, getting a result, seeing 'fruit for our labours'. We are in the race to win, not just to run (1 Corinthians 9:24).

So we need some goals. I've found that, to be effective, they need to be:

● *Agreed.* They can't be imposed without consultation. A goal without a supporting team becomes an own-goal! Don't expect unanimity but help people to share 'ownership' of the goals as much as possible. *Our* goals may be met, goals which are *theirs* won't be.

● *Shared.* Don't get a goal in view and then take your eye off the ball! Concentrate on the issue, tell others what progress is being made, share the positives, keep people up to date.

• *Achievable*. Goals must stretch faith but not snap it! 'Fifty new converts this Sunday' is certainly a laudable goal, but if your present congregation has only twenty members, it probably won't be a goal with much faith in it. Start small. New, more difficult goals can be set once you have achieved the easier ones.

• *Measurable*. Will you know when you have met it? The goal could be measured in pounds, numbers of people, numbers of activities etc, but it must be clear and definite. You can't score if you keep moving the goal posts.

• *Reviewed*. Regular assessments must take place. Are we achieving our goal? If so, what's next? If not, what are the reasons for our failure? Perhaps the goal was unrealistic or we didn't allow enough time to accomplish it. We learn more from failure to reach our goals than in succeeding, *if* we do this hard analytical reviewing. However, never let the failure to reach a goal be the occasion for apportioning 'blame'. This breeds a negative, critical spirit, hardly conducive to setting other faith goals in the future.

Almost all of church life would benefit from having faith-goals. Perhaps we could pray and work for two new house groups this year, a fifteen per cent rise in the offerings, ten new members and the establishment of a worship group. Perhaps we could have goals which would take two or three years – buy the minister a new car, increase the church staff or completely redecorate the building. Whatever we decide to go for . . . let's go for it!

Goals can be faith in action. God calls us to have faith. We have exercised it for our personal salvation, shall we exercise it less as we look to God for the growth of his church?

> 'Give me the faith which can remove
> And sink the mountain to a plain;
> Give me the childlike, praying love.
> Which longs to build Thy house again;
> Thy love, let it my heart o'erpower,
> Let it my ransomed soul devour.'
> *Charles Wesley*

6

Communication: Seeing is Believing

THE ISSUES

Constant change is here to stay! And not only is change going to be an ever-present part of our cultural landscape but the rate of change is going to increase. This rapidly changing world poses significant problems for governments and multi-national industries; no wonder it's a problem for local churches!

Community in a visual age

One of the most significant things which has been affected by all this change is the business of communication – how we send and receive information. Obviously the church is in the business of trying to send out some pretty significant information! We believe that we have the best piece of news ever and we have been told by God to broadcast it as widely as possible. Sadly, the vast majority of churches are transmitting the message on some obscure, short-wave radio frequency while the world is watching *Neighbours*! We are communicating to the very rare individual who happens to have the equipment and inclination to tune in – the vast majority of the population have neither.

The mention of *Neighbours* illustrates one of the most telling changes in the way communication is received today. During the last fifty years, television has revolutionised our lives; it has shaped our view of the world, changed the face of politics and transformed our understanding of 'entertainment'. People now expect to 'see' their information in moving images, rather than simply read print or listen to spoken words. Nearly every home has at least one set, and it seems to have an almost addictive power. Whether we like it or not this is the kind of world into which the church must take its message.

A church left behind

There was a minister of a church who had a magnificent collection of slides of sunsets from all over the world. Showing them to an admiring, but bemused, audience, he was asked how he came to have such a marvellous array of scenes, as they had not known he had ever travelled outside his own country.

'Well, actually', he smiled, 'they're not mine. They belong to as many people as there are slides. You see, we have missionaries on deputation coming to our church once every few months, and they all show us slides of their work. And it's interesting how many of them finish up with a slide of a local sunset, saying, "and as the sun sets on Limpopoland, do remember us in our ministry there . . ." As they pack up their slides, displays, handouts and prayer letters, they nearly always leave the last slide in the church's projector! They're not bad, are they?'

If it weren't so near the truth, such a story could be funny. But to make the cliché even worse, the archetypal church or missionary meeting has the screen that won't stand upright, the projector bulb that blows, the forgotten extension cord (so that there is either a tiny picture on a huge wall, or else a huge picture spreading outside the screen onto the tatty velvet curtains on the stage behind), the hymn books propping up the projector on a rickety flower stand, and the series of slides of 'me with the village elders', or 'me at the local market place'.

The problem facing the church is that the caricature of amateurish means of communication, often limited to the spoken or written word, is too close to the truth for comfort. And yet we live in a world and in an age where communication has become a major growth industry. Marshall McLuhan's 'the medium is the message' is now old hat, as the wonders of the electronic age have further shrunk the 'global village' that was such a radical concept when it was first launched in the sixties.

Expectations and attention spans

Generally, people expect to be met with a much higher standard of communication than most local churches are yet delivering. The battle is lost almost before it is fought. With television, cinema and video part of everyday life, even in some remote African villages, homely little homilies and soporific sermons, pale into insignificance.

The average teenager watches twenty-eight hours of television a week. By the time he leaves school, he will have watched 22,000 hours of television and seen 5000 feature length movies. The average working person watches over eighteen hours of television programmes a week: more than two working days' worth of viewing. By the time the average televiewer has reached sixty years of age, that person has spent nine years of life in front of the television screen.

Viewers are trained to have limited attention time. Scenes are cut into seconds rather than minutes, and commercial breaks (even on non-commercial channels) come between sections far shorter than the average sermon. Is it any wonder that even twenty minutes of monologue drives church members to counting the bricks in the wall behind the pulpit, or calculating various permutations and combinations of the hymn numbers!

People are also accustomed to variety, to having their emotions touched, to being passive viewers rather than active participants. Is it surprising, therefore, that televised church and religious hymn programmes are enormously popular? How can the local pastor compete and, indeed, should she or he even try?

Being contemporary

We've come a long way since flannelgraphs, but there still often seems to be a Christian reserve about using modern techniques of communication and of aiming for excellence or professionalism. It is almost as if 'anything goes' when it comes to church, while in the world only the best will do. At the same time, however, more and more churches are taking advantage of the benefits that computers and word processors can offer, whether for providing data bases of church members, for sermon preparation and editing, or as filing systems for illustrations and stories. The thought of using modern communication methods, perhaps involving different styles of music, or dance and the visual arts, is still an offence to many traditionalists – whether in worship or theology – though they dearly love the Lord and his church.

Music
At one time when we were living in New Zealand, we were visited by an aunt from Australia, a keen Christian who played the organ at her local church. We found a church of her denomination (or so we thought) for us all to attend together during her stay. When we arrived, however, we found there was no organ, as that particular group felt it was unbiblical and worldly to have any musical accompaniment to the hymn singing.

In itself, there is nothing wrong with having no accompaniment to singing. I have been in parts of Africa and the South Pacific where, without accompaniment, and with a single note sung to lead off, a whole congregation has burst into paeans of praise in perfect eight-part harmony, and with much joy! Such was not the case in the New Zealand church. It was painful. And I felt supercilious and critical of their narrow shortsightedness.

However, I have not always been as positive as I might have been. It was not too many years after the New Zealand incident that we were pastoring a growing church in Sydney, Australia. The evening congregation was enthusiastic and open to new ideas and wanted a music group to lead the worship. There were a number of gifted instrumentalists and singers, and they had my warm encouragement – until the drums arrived. Were they really appropriate for church? What about the link with African tribalism, and the evils of rock and roll? And what would the older members of the congregation think? Even the trumpet was somewhat intrus-ive. And what about the organist, who insisted we needed the highest quality of church organ music to make our worship acceptable to God?

I had not thought much about Lucifer at that stage of my ministry, but I was becoming increasingly convinced that, before he became a fallen angel, he must have been an organ-ist, or a choirmaster – or at the very least a musician of *some* kind! I mean no offence by such a sweeping statement – some of my best friends, including my own children, are musicians! But the regularity with which music seems to cause division and strife in the church is surely more than coincidental.

The arts in worship

Similarly, the slowness and suspicion with which the arts generally are welcomed in Christian circles, seems inconsist-ent with the mass of biblical material which would seem to validate their wide use. During our time in England we have come to know just some of those believers who are gifted in the arts, and have shared in the new experience (to us) of the big events such as Spring Harvest and Greenbelt where thousands gather together to grapple with gospel issues. The arts receive a higher than average exposure in such settings but, even so, we have met hurt, disillusionment, a sense of rejection, misunderstanding and marginalisation on the part of the artists themselves.

One of them, a poet, recounted to us a regular conversation he has when he meets Christian people for the first time. 'And what do you do?' 'I'm a poet.' 'Yes, but what do you *do*?' 'I write poetry.' 'But how do you earn your living?' 'I actually depend on writing poetry!' 'Really?' And the subject quickly switches to something more manageable, like the weather.

Generally speaking, 'normal' Christians, if there are such creatures, do seem to feel that anything to do with the arts is sinister and diabolic at worst, or wordly at best. An experi-enced evangelist recounted the tale of his conversion to Christ in a little Welsh chapel. Having settled matters with God at the penitent's rail, before he left the gathering he was given a sheet of paper on which were listed sixteen points, all to be avoided by young Christian men who wished to take their discipleship seriously. They ranged from the predictable drinking of alcohol and smoking, through playing cards and gambling, going to the cinema (videos did not exist in those days), dancing, and even specifying the number of inches within which one must not approach a member of the opposite sex!

Being biblical

Admittedly, times have changed. Many might say the pendulum has swung too far in the opposite direction. But the fact that use of the arts in worship is still very limited in this country is indicative of the hesitation in Christian circles to see them as valid means of communicating the gospel. Of course, distinctions need to be drawn – for instance, between 'dancing' and 'dancing'. Even in the Bible, a certain kind of dancing, such as that of Herodias' daughter before the beheading of John the Baptist (Mark 6:22), could not be described as spiritually uplifting!

However, if we look at history, contemporary experience and the Bible, as well as Jesus' own communication methods, we find more than ample justification for making use of a wide variety of communication methods, both in worship and in the church's wider links with society.

Pictures as well as words

Historically, the church made much capital out of the visual presentation of the good news, not least in extended periods when very few people could read. Stained glass windows bear testimony to that fact, as do the miracle and morality plays of the Middle Ages. It is a sober reminder for those who lay such store by the printed word – invaluable though it is, not least because of its relative permanence – to realise that the church only survived during the Dark Ages because the faith could be effectively communicated by means other than print.

The Bible abounds with imaginative communication methods. Weird though some of them may seem, Ezekiel's dramas certainly stay in the mind. Others of God's prophets had vivid and memorable pictorial visions – Amos, Zechariah and John the Divine amongst them. The latter's images of persecution, catastrophe, spiritual warfare and heaven have been the staple diet of eschatologists down through the centuries. And how often have King David's portrayal of God as the good shepherd, and Jesus' many real-life illustrations, brought back to mind biblical truths more effectively than abstract concepts ever have?

Expressive and adventurous music

The contemporary church has seen a plethora of song books and worship leaders, of music groups and dance fellowships. In the face of Christian conservatism that views these with suspicion, we should ask Cliff Richard's question, 'Why should the devil have all the good music?' Why indeed, particularly when the Bible puts such emphasis on expressive and adventurous music: 'Sing for joy to God our strength, shout aloud to the God of Jacob!' wrote David (Psalm 81:1). To do so in some of our churches would be thought 'unseemly' or irreverent. It might even be discouraged.

After the miraculous crossing of the Red Sea and the defeat of the Egyptian Pharaoh, Miriam 'took a tambourine in her hand, and all the women followed her, with tambourines and dancing' (Exodus 15:20). If it was acceptable for Miriam the prophetess, no less a person than Moses' sister, to worship God by joyful singing and dancing at such a high point in Israel's history, it is surely equally so for us today.

David himself, rejoicing to bring the sacred ark of God into Jerusalem, 'danced before the Lord with all his might, while he and the entire house of Israel brought up the ark of the Lord with shouts and the sound of trumpets' (2 Samuel 6:14–15). David also told the leaders of the Levites to 'appoint their brothers as singers to sing joyful songs, accompanied by musical instruments: lyres, harps and cymbals' (1 Chronicles 15:16).

So there is good biblical justification for a lavish and exciting use of music, instruments and dancing, as part of our joyful expression of the faith, in praise and thanksgiving. If the church is to relate to the world where the media are so influential, such adventurousness in music could make an attractive impression.

Symbols and stories

The greatest communicator of all time must be Jesus. Who apart from him could have made such a timeless impact with such limited resources in such an amazingly brief three year period of public ministry? Who else could have died such a shameful, criminal's death, only to have the means of execution become a permanent, instantly recognisable symbol of the faith he founded?

And here lies one of Jesus's secrets. He used stories, symbols, illustrations and signs to communicate in a striking and astonishingly permanent way: the towel he used to wash the disciples' feet; the bread and the wine to represent his body and blood about to be given up so soon after that fateful Last Supper; the memorable parables, like the Good Samaritan and the Prodigal Son; the pithy statements such as 'it is easier for a camel to go through the eye of a needle than for a rich man to enter the kingdom of God' (Matthew 19:24), and the multitude of homely, earthy illustrations that struck such a chord in the hearts, minds and wills of his hearers.

If we, his contemporary disciples, are to make any inroads into our increasingly secularised, disillusioned and sense-sated world, we need to learn our lesson well, and make use of all the sanctified skills, gifts and abilities available to us, the arts included.

THE WAY FORWARD

Ground rules

How, in practice, can local congregations respond to the increasingly 'visual' world of the twentieth century? First, we need to understand and help the church family work through the following.

● *Adapting to these changes in our society is not 'wordly'!* The feeling that making changes would be to become 'worldly' is the biggest hurdle for many congregations. We need to recognise that the gospel message itself is unchanging but the packaging it comes in *must* keep on changing. Jesus presented his message in quite different ways depending on his audience, and Paul used totally different techniques in different cultural settings. It is imperative that we learn from this. Most of our buildings, organisations and structures have their roots in another generation. They may have been appropriate *then* but they can be positive barriers *now*: they are not part of the biblical mandate – we may replace them if we want to!

● *Adapting to these changes in our world is not 'unspiritual'* – nor does it deny God's ability to speak to people through anything he might choose to. This criticism is similar to the last one. It comes into the 'if God had meant us to fly in planes he would never have invented trains' kind of logic. 'God is all-powerful and he has used the pipe organ/*King James' Version*/pews in the past; are you saying he can't use it now?' Well, of course not, but what's the point of making it more difficult for twentieth century people than it needs to

be? If they can't relate to these means of conveying the message, we need to find new means.

The gospel must never be made easier to respond to by diluting its *demands*; the simple truth is offensive to some. But this does not mean that the packaging needs to be unattractive, nor should it make it more difficult to *understand* the gospel. There is nothing spiritual in disguising the power and beauty of the message by presenting it in a form only someone in another generation could relate to!

• *We must be driven to these changes by purpose not 'novelty'.* Things must change because we desperately want to communicate with modern men and women; not merely because we like trying something new! Most congregations are much more sympathetic to change if they can identify a clear purpose rather than thinking we are jumping on some bandwagon. It is amazing, for example, how many churches bought a computer in the mid 1980s without having the slightest idea what to use it for! It just seemed a good idea at the time.

• *We must distinguish carefully between tradition and traditionalism.* Tradition is the living faith of the dead; traditionalism is the dead faith of the living. The former must be honoured, cherished and preserved; the latter can be discarded as an unnecessary encumbrance for the task in hand. We must help our churches discern the difference or we risk mistakes at both ends of the argument. For example, we could decide that harvest festivals are a relic from the agricultural era, and have no place in modern church life. After all, in the vast majority of cases, people work in offices and factories, not on farms! 'So let's scrap them.' Actually, I think this is a mistake. Many non-Christians see harvest festivals as a significant part of their heritage and see a role for the church in it. However, it will remain of historical interest unless a fax machine, mobile phone, car jack and stethoscope (for example) appear in the display along with the fruit and vegetables – a token of giving our work back to God. In addition, the 'food' aspect of harvest can be rescued from traditionalism by addressing such themes as the environmental crisis, world hunger and the spiritual hunger which God can fill.

So, in the case of harvest, the *idea* may come in the category 'tradition' and the *form* of the service in the category 'traditionalism'. When we get the distinction between the two right, we run far less risk of jettisoning the valuable or retaining the unimportant!

As the church begins to work through these principles in leaders' meetings, house groups and informal discussion, attitudes begin to change. Business people who have had to implement massive changes in their places of work, will suddenly wake up to a similar need in the church. People will start questioning the way they receive information themselves and hopefully begin to put themselves in the position of others who don't share their faith. 'If I wasn't a Christian what would I think of my church? What "message" are we communicating to them?' Questions like these pave the way for some practical changes.

Church buildings

What message do our buildings send out? Would you go inside if you didn't have to?! Our buildings are seen by everyone who walks or drives past them and by our immediate neighbours. Probably thousands more see our premises than visit them on a Sunday. If they communicate 'derelict' or 'drab' or 'dark' then we are obviously putting off casual visitors. The ideal is a light, clean building which you can see inside. If you can have a welcoming person at an obvious reception point, so much the better. Remember that the visual impact is crucial. Many people in your community will work in light, open-plan offices in modern buildings. Imagine the 'feel' of your church building to them.

Of course, most church buildings can't be demolished and rebuilt! Even extensive remodelling is often too costly. But can it be thoroughly cleaned, given a new coat of paint, even lit in a more effective way? Could litter be cleared regularly, the grounds tidied up and the railings repaired? Of course, a large, clear notice board helps communicate life and activity. Keep the wording simple and brief and change it regularly.

And think creatively . . . anything to help make the building look user-friendly. Could you put up some kind of brightly coloured awning? Have you got enough ground for a small, all-weather play area? A covered area with seats and perhaps a picnic table? None of these ideas may be right for your church – but something will be! Encourage people to use their imaginations.

And what about once we get inside our buildings? What sights greet our eyes? Once again, redecoration may be part of the answer, particularly in the vestibule – what people see in the first few seconds colours their attitude to almost everything else. Clean, light, warm and 'inviting' is the aim. Posters and banners tastefully arranged, some comfy chairs perhaps, background music, a 'welcome desk' all these things can help people begin to relax and feel at home. We may be able to serve coffee – in new mugs not slightly stained china cups – and biscuits (preferably less than a year old!). How about coffee and jam doughnuts *before* the service? We could provide somewhere to hang coats, cloakrooms with a mirror, and soft toilet paper! All these things might seem trivial but their absence communicates a negative message to people living at the end of the twentieth century.

Church services

Television has heightened people's expectations of quality in performance. The rapid-fire, high quality programmes they enjoy night by night are tough to compete with. Even the news uses a variety of techniques to hold attention: studio guests, video clips, diagrams and maps, the news reader – and all in two-minute bursts! Most presentations of Sunday services seem dull by comparison. How can we communicate to a generation of people who have grown used to this visual feast at the touch of a button? Well, we could try:

● *Drama*. This can be very effective even when the script and the actors fall short of Shakespearean standards! Aim for excellence but don't wait until you achieve it before using the drama group. A dramatic two/three voice reading of the Bible can be very effective. Most groups can re-enact a parable and, with experience, will be able to add their own touches of pathos and humour. There is a lot of good material

about for drama groups to use. Bad drama is an embarrassment but good, simple drama adds a wonderful visual
element to any service.

• *Poetry*. Most poetry written by church members is pretty
dire; the rest of it is worse! There is some excellent published
Christian poetry around though; read well, it can touch the
emotions and grant insights which prose fails to give. It can
be used as part of worship or in teaching. Should you stumble
across a poet of quality in your congregation, encourage and
use him or her.

• *Mime and dance*. Very difficult to do well, but hard-
working enthusiasts in local churches have been known to
add a special dimension to worship by these means. Special-
ists can sometimes be invited in to 'demonstrate' the value of
these art forms in worship and even begin to train a group
of potential performers.

• *Visual aids*. Video is great if you can get a pertinent clip
onto a large enough screen! Slides can be a super asset to a
worship time if accompanied by music, a passage from the
Bible or prayers (with eyes open!). Remember to use your
overhead projector for pictures as well as words for songs.
Cartoons on the overhead can stimulate interest, make a
telling point and create laughter – all at the same time!

• *Music*. We can encourage instrumentalists to play sensitively during some of the prayers and readings. If we have
competent soloists we can use them; if not, a cassette of an
appropriate song (with the words on the overhead projector)
can be very stimulating.

We can also develop the strengths that exist in our services
in the things which they provide and which are *lacking* in
television communication – silence, interaction and response,
for example. We will look at some of these issues in chapter
eight.

Nevertheless, we must recognise that our society is used to
pace, variety, humour, colour, movement and energy from
its television screens. Church buildings and church services
are in danger of communicating a message which remains
obscured by a slow-moving, repetitive, humourless, monochrome, passive and lifeless 'package'! God help us to set his

Son free from these communication chains so that at least in the twenty-first century people will be making their minds up about the message *itself* – because we have actually got through to them with what it is all about.

> 'I want to serve the purpose of God
>   in my generation.
> I want to serve the purpose of God
>   while I am alive.
> I want to give my life to something
>   that will last forever.
> Oh, I delight, I delight to do Your will.'

I WANT TO SERVE THE PURPOSE
Mark Altrogge
Copyright © 1982 People of Destiny/Thankyou Music
PO Box 75, Eastbourne, East Sussex, BN23 6NW, UK
Used by permission

7

Preaching:
Getting the Message

THE ISSUES

The graffiti scrawled on the walls of the Paris metro stated baldly the familiar Christian cliché: 'Jesus Christ is the answer.' Underneath it was the poignant rejoinder, 'What was the question?'

Questions about the meaning and purpose of life are being asked today, both inside and outside the church, perhaps more openly than ever before. The various answers that people are being given have led many to disillusionment and, at times, fear. The sad reality is that the church is guilty of spending a good deal of time answering questions that no-one is asking any more, and in a way that seems not only irrelevant, but boring, dull, confusing, drawn out, longwinded, monotonous and empty. We have looked in the last chapter at the need to smarten up the visual element in our communication; now we turn our attention to the verbal – and, particularly, to the sermon.

The message at the heart of the gospel is that of Jesus – the living Word and the bread of life. It is vital food that the church needs to make available to people, and there are two key areas that we need to get straight in order to do so.

Powerful preaching

A preacher once said from the pulpit to a woman in the congregation, 'Would you mind waking up that man next to you?' She smiled and answered, 'You wake him up. You put him to sleep!'

On another occasion, a Scottish Presbyterian had been soundly berating his congregation for almost an hour. As he pounded the pulpit in a dramatic climax, he asked the hypothetical question in soaring oratorical tones: 'What more can I say?' A wag in the back pew responded, 'Och aye, mon; say "amen" and sit doon!'

The day of preaching is not over. However, the quality of preaching, let alone the variety of other means of communication used, often leaves much to be desired. New emphasis is being given to training in sound, biblical teaching – which is good; but even here the danger is that the cerebral approach will exclude the emotions. Both are essential and need to be combined creatively to get the message across in a powerful way.

The medium and the message

Once again, Jesus is our model. He was a magnificent communicator, involving the mind, the emotions and the will, and demanding a response from his hearers. This ought not to surprise us, for John's opening description in his Gospel makes it clear that Jesus was not only the supreme *means* of communication by which God chose to make himself known to his creation, but he was also the *message*, the content of the good news:

'In the beginning was the Word, and the Word was with God, and the Word was God . . . The Word became flesh and lived for a while among us. We have seen his glory, the glory of the One and only, who came from the Father, full of grace and truth' (John 1:1, 14).

The whole gamut of human emotions was involved in God's communication process, as Jesus lived the life of a human being. We will never crack the mystery of how God could become man, or of how Jesus and God can be one, but we can understand enough to know that Jesus had feelings. He wept, knew tiredness, experienced anger, felt compassion and was troubled (see John 11:35; 4:6; 2:16; Mark 1:41; John 12:27). It was not just by word, spoken or written, that God spoke.

In the same way, it is by who we are, not just by what what we say or do, that we communicate the message. 'I can't hear what you're saying, because what you're doing drowns out your words,' challenges us to the integrity of life demanded of all Jesus' disciples. How much more does it apply to those with the privilege of publicly preaching the word?

The creative word

Way back at creation God's speaking was dynamically creative. Listen to the dramatic account:

> 'And God said, "Let there be light", and there was light . . . And God said, "Let there be an expanse between the waters to separate water from water . . . God called the expanse sky . . .' (Genesis 1:3, 6, 8).

And as God continued speaking, creation came into being: the dry land, vegetation, night and day, water creatures, birds, animals and, finally, man and woman. What a breathtaking crescendo! What visual aids! And not without its touch of humour either. Who, without a profound sense of fun, could have come up with such quirky oddities as the giraffe and the platypus, the ostrich and the camel – and you and me?

One of the problems the church has made for itself as it has tried to communicate the good news, is that it has so often failed to use words creatively. God has given us the gift of speech not just to transmit bland information, but to reach people's emotions, fire their imaginations and move their wills to respond to him. What a difference there would be in many churches today if communicators and preachers tried some innovations, learned some new skills, and showed creativity and imagination in their use of the sermon!

A Bible-based message

My experience from observations in many countries is that

where the Bible is taken seriously by a church as God's word for them today, that church is alive. If we want to see our churches die in a decade, the quickest way to effect their demise is to remove the Bible from that central point in their lives. If we want life and growth, we will make sure that the Bible is the basis of our preaching and teaching ministry, that its message is applied in a relevant way to the lives of our congregation, and that preacher and hearers alike humbly submit to what God has to say to us through it. On some issues, the possibility of a number of different interpretations will call for honesty and clarity of thought, an openness to hearing God speak to us in ways we had not expected, and a willingness to listen to one another's views. The Bible is powerful. We can let it loose in our churches with a sense of great anticipation!

The fears and dangers

Having spent a good part of my life firstly with the Bible Society, and latterly with Scripture Union, as well as having been involved predominantly in a preaching, teaching and speaking ministry, I am well aware of the dangers of a narrow and restricted use of the Bible.

● *'Bibliolatry.'* Firstly, 'bibliolatry' is close to the surface for many evangelicals. The words themselves (often the King James' version!) can become so special to them that the concepts behind them can be abused or misused, hiding the Lord whom they are meant to reveal.

George Carey, in an interview prior to his enthronement as Archbishop of Canterbury, said,

'I believe that most evangelicals are not Scripture people at all – they have a tendency to put a "construct" on Scripture and treat it as a wax nose which is pushed and pulled into any direction they wish. Many are secretly afraid to expose themselves to critical insights because they fear that if they do so, they will surrender doctrines of inerrancy and infallibility. If this is their secret fear, then they are right. The tendency therefore is to become slightly heretical in that Scripture is placed higher than Christ.' (George Carey, quoted in *Today*, August 1990.)

• *'Selective hermeneutics'* Secondly, this worshipping of the word rather than the Word, Jesus, can lead to 'selective hermeneutics': verses, phrases or words are interpreted – often taken out of context – in a way that bolsters a personal hobby horse. It arises because the interpreter is more concerned to see himself proved right than he is to put himself before the bar of Scripture.

I came across an extreme example of 'selective hermeneutics' in an area of the South Pacific. There, if a pastor is widowed, he has to remarry within a year, or he loses his ordination. The justification for this interesting custom is 1 Timothy 3:2 which says: 'The overseer must be above reproach, the husband of but one wife . . .' The fact that the *meaning* is clearly, 'not the husband of more than one wife' is immaterial. The literalism leads to the absurd.

A more controversial selectivity comes in the previous chapter, where Paul states unequivocally: 'I do not permit a woman to teach or to have authority over a man, she must be silent' (1 Timothy 2:12). An amazing variety of church practices have been based on this verse, most of them disregarding the absurdity of the 'silence' if taken literally, and the fact that Paul had numbers of woman co-workers who taught and ministered effectively, and with his grateful encouragement (see Romans 16).

Opponents of women's ministry will say that the meaning of Scripture is perfectly clear: women must not teach or speak but keep silent in church. The illogical – or is it disobedient? – use of women in singing, reading of the Scriptures, in establishing churches in missionary situations and leading fellowship groups, is apparently not seen as being inconsistent. And when challenged on the meaning of 1 Timothy 2:15, 'women will be saved through childbearing', such folk have come up with a bewildering variety of interpretations.

We need, then, to beware of bibliolatry in preaching, and of arrogance in our use of the Bible. It is not our word, but the word of God. It is 'living and active. Sharper than any double-edged sword, it penetrates even to dividing soul and spirit, joints and marrow; it judges the thoughts and attitudes of the heart' (Hebrews 4:12).

If our churches are to come to life and grow, our preaching

ministry must be based on the Bible, but we must be sure that it is Christ centred. It is, after all, on Christ that the whole Bible focuses – from Genesis to Revelation. The Old Testament prepares the way for Jesus, and the New Testament reveals him; he is the hinge between BC and AD on which the whole of world history swings. If this is the whole thrust of the Bible, can that of our preaching be anything less?

'I'm no expert, Joe, but perhaps you shouldn't close each sermon with "But then again, what do I know?" '

The Bible's centrality in the lives of individuals

If the medium is the message – or at least, a powerful part of the message conveyed – then the attitude of the congregation towards that message is a significant factor in how seriously it is taken by those outside the church. Our congregations need to rediscover the truth that the Bible is God's word for them, now, and so take the study and reading of it seriously. Small groups of church members who meet together regularly to study the Bible and to pray are the lifeblood of the church.

In order to keep the Bible's teaching central to our church life we will need to encourage individual members of the fellowship to read the Bible enthusiastically, systematically and daily. For those who struggle to read, there are cassettes designed to help the listener into the Bible each day and to listen to God through it. Such daily discipline can, of course, be hard work, and our encouragement of each other is vital.

We also need to encourage the reading of Christian literature to help people understand and apply the Bible's teaching. There is power and permanence in the printed word. It is sobering for preachers to realise how small a percentage of their message is recalled even by lunch time on Sunday, let alone by Monday! Tape recordings of sermons help keep them alive in people's minds, but the printed word can reach 'where no other methods can.'

It is amazing how many regular church attenders see no need for any spiritual nourishment other than the weekly dose of a sermon. People think they can stoke up at church for the week much as they fill their cars once a week with petrol. But the human body doesn't work like that, neither does the human soul! We need regular, daily bread to live healthy and productive spiritual lives. This lack of regular spiritual feeding, endemic in our churches, has led us into superficial, malnourished Christian living. As a result, God's people have all too often absorbed and reflected the values and lifestyle of the secular society in which they find themselves. The distinctiveness to which God's people are called – to be 'in the world but not of it' – can only come from a nourished and intimate relationship with God.

In his book, *Celebration of Discipline* (London: Hodder and Stoughton, 1989), Richard Foster outlines the part that spiritual disciplines play in Christian growth, seeing them as the doors to liberated service. He divides them into three: the inward disciplines (meditation, prayer, fasting and study), the outward disciplines (simplicity, solitude, submission and service), and the corporate disciplines (confession, worship, guidance and celebration).

Foster's assertion is that true liberation is found only as a result of discipline. A musician, for instance, doesn't have the freedom to play demanding symphonies and concertos without the long hours of disciplined practice. This turns upside-down the prevailing thought of the age, that freedom comes only from throwing off tradition, which is seen as a shackle that binds, restricts and oppresses. And yet the phrase in the old *Book of Common Prayer*, 'in whose service is perfect freedom', captures the reality of a life disciplined in order to be more completely available to God. The study and meditation of the Bible is an essential ingredient in this.

A practice which seems to have almost died out today, though it was an integral part of the spiritual life of earlier generations of Christians, is that of the 'quiet time', otherwise known affectionately as the 'QT'. It is simply a period of time set aside daily for prayer and Bible reading, normally in the morning before the day gets under way. Its popularity has declined over recent years partly because, for some people, it degenerated into a kind of spiritual insurance policy: if you did the Scripture Union reading, mentally answering the questions of the Scripture Union method, quickly read notes and said a brief prayer relating the passage to the day's activities, then your day would go well. God would bless you! But if you got up late, had to gobble down your breakfast then run out for the train without so much as a glance in the direction of your Bible, then you'd better look out! God wouldn't be very pleased with you. For others it became a legalistic chore, loading them with a heavy sense of guilt and inferiority if they found it hard to set aside this time. But for some, it remains a precious daily experience that nourishes and fosters their living relationship with God. It is unhurried time set aside to hear him clearly through his word, to listen to him and to pray.

We can easily understand the reaction against the legalism that led to the 'quiet time' being gradually abandoned. But I fear it is another instance of throwing the baby out with the bathwater. It has meant that a new and younger generation has come into being in the church for whom the Bible is peripheral, and for whom, in their worlds of frenetic activity, prayer and meditation are unfamiliar. This can only result in a superficial spirituality based on what *I* feel or what *I* think, rather than what *God* wants of me.

How, then, do we put into practice these twin aspects of getting the message across: effective preaching and a Bible-based, Christ-centred message?

THE WAY FORWARD

Getting the message

'I've listened to you chatting, preacher, chatting from
    your heart,
But didn't dig your message 'cause you lost me at the start.
I'm sure you said them from your heart, the things you
    had to say
But heart is not sufficient if your lips get in the way.'

Gordon Bailey

What preacher has not had a problem with his lips getting
in the way? How can we make the best use of this means of
communication in an age dominated by the television?

Let's be under no illusions. Preachers in the last decade of
the twentieth century face some stiff opposition, not least
from the 'box in the corner'. Are you as 'warm' as Wogan,
as witty as Clive James and as believable as Alastair Burnett?
Subconscious comparisons are going on in the minds of our
congregations! And what's more, they may well have been
to hear a famous preacher the night before who is 'on tour'
or watched a video of another equally famous speaker or
been listening to his cassettes in the car on the way to work.
So, here you are at 11am on a Sunday morning, seeing if
you can compete with the secular and spiritual giants of
communication. So far, so discouraging!

Of course, as a local preacher you do have some advantages: you can address community needs, relate to individuals
you know and apply your material to specific situations. No
television personality or visiting Christian celebrity can come
near your abilities in these areas.

In addition, all of us can think carefully about our communication skills and the vast majority of us can improve
our presentations significantly. But how?

Think visual!
As we have already noted, people in recent years have become
very 'eye dependant'. They concentrate better, and for longer,
if there is something to look at. Use the overhead projector,
at least for your text and main points. Use some of the
creative arts at various points in the message (see previous

100

chapter). You are your own best (or worst) visual aid: think carefully about what you wear. Don't be boring, but remember that over-zany or ultra-bright clothing can be a distraction! And don't forget movement and gesture – be natural but be animated.

Learn from the TV studio. It is relatively uncluttered so that the focus of the eye is always being drawn to the presenters. Avoid visual distractions near the place where you are speaking; anything with a bit of colour or a pattern is likely to be more interesting than you are! If things can't be moved, lighting can often be used to make you stand out from your surroundings.

Think variety!

An image seldom remains on screen for more than a few seconds. People are used to having their attention held by a rapid sequence of different pictures. Our preaching needs to reflect something of this variety try to vary these elements:

Variety in voice: sometimes loud, occasionally little more than a whisper, and the effective use of pauses.

Variety in content: take exegesis and exposition, thoroughly mix with application; bring quickly to the boil with passion and pathos. Sprinkle liberally with illustrations and quotations and pour in the sauce of humour for added taste. Garnish with a smile. Serve with relish!

Variety in approach: perhaps a topical sermon, rather than exposition of a passage. Perhaps you could preach twice in the service (for half as long!), or encourage questions at the end. 'Plant' a heckler in the congregation or break for a couple of minutes of group discussion.

Think response!

The success of recent 'telethons' has been amazing; thousands of people have given millions of pounds in response to these televised appeals. It's a relatively simple formula: attention and interest are gained, usually through music or comedy; the need is described clearly and graphically and a simple response encouraged – 'ring this number'. And people do!

This technique is not new. Jesus, the ultimate communicator, would often grab people's attention with a statement or action they weren't expecting, and follow this up with an explanation and an invitation to respond. We are looking to see lives changed through our preaching – people responding to what we have said. This means, of course, that we must make it clear what we are expecting people to *do* as a result of what they have just heard. Visually-oriented and variety-filled sermons are the building blocks of good preaching, not the goal of preaching; which is to build a house which people will move into! Preaching in the pulpit must lead to action in the pew.

The preacher

The previous paragraphs are based on some assumptions. They assume that we are keen to communicate to the world as it is, not as it was fifty years ago; that we want our message to be heard and understood by modern men and women and that we are prepared to work hard at this aspect of the art of preaching. As Martin Lloyd-Jones wrote, some twenty years ago, 'I would say that a "dull preacher" is a contradiction in terms; if he is dull he is not a preacher.'

Also assumed is the need for prayerful preparation and careful study. No amount of communication technique can replace a systematic analysis of God's word in the study and a thoughtful exposition of it in the pulpit. The Bible still has its ancient power; let loose, it will still accomplish supernatural results.

In addition, though the skills and ideas described above are very important, they are not the *most* important things. These *most* important things would include openness to God's Spirit and faithfulness to his word.

As we approach the twenty-first century, we are confronted with two desperate needs.

Genuine passion

We need preachers with genuine passion – not pedlars of sentiment and emotionalism which masquerade as passion, but men and women with fire in their bellies and hearts overflowing with love for a lost world; people sold out to the task of bringing sinners to salvation and saints to maturity through their preaching. John Stott puts it this way,

'I constantly find myself wishing that we twentieth-century

preachers could learn to weep again. But either our tear-springs have dried up, or our tear-ducts have become blocked. Everything seems to conspire together to make it impossible for us to cry over lost sinners who throng the broad road which leads to destruction.' (John Stott, *I Believe in Preaching*, London: Hodder, 1982.)

A sense of awe

We need preachers with a sense of awe. Much preaching caricatures this holy calling. We need more preachers to have a genuine fear of God, a healthy view of their own unworthiness and a deep sense of humility. God help us if we are merely slick communicators who can produce a professional performance! We need to be those who can echo the words Martin Luther used to pray before he preached:

> 'Lord God, you have made me a pastor in your church. You see how unfit I am to undertake this great and difficult office, and if it were not for your help, I would have ruined it all long ago. Therefore I cry to you for aid. I offer my mouth and my heart to your service. I desire to teach the people – and for myself, I would learn evermore and diligently meditate on your word. Use me as your instrument, but never forsake me, for if I am left alone I shall easily bring it all to destruction. Amen.'

Using the Bible

The Bible is not only the foundation of all our preaching but it must permeate all aspects of church life. Congregations, as well as preachers, must move on from paying lip-service to the importance of scripture, to actually demonstrating it. Of course, church leaders have a major role to play here; if they are obviously getting their sermons from the Bible, using its teaching as the basis for church decisions and for planning their own lives, the congregation is likely to follow their lead. So how can we release the Bible from being trapped in Mark Twain's definition of a classic, '. . . a book everyone wants to have read and no-one wants to read!'? Here are some ideas:

Encourage private use

Ordinary Christians must be encouraged to read, study, meditate on and memorise the Bible. You may be able to stimulate interest by having people give public testimony to their own growth through their private meditation on the Bible, or through writing an article for the church magazine or running a seminar on 'How to get the best out of your Bible'.

We can develop our knowledge and love of the Bible in other ways too. Commentaries and study guides can open up whole areas of truth to us which we can explore. Bible meditation with a friend can be an exciting adventure as scripture yields its secrets to this combination of reading, prayer and fellowship. Or why not give several hours to reading a whole Bible book in one sitting? Or spend one hour meditating on one verse?

Do stress that there is no 'set' method or time for this; encourage people to be creative in their approach to it. For instance, not everyone is a lark, at their most awake first thing in the morning; or an owl, more lively late at night. Some may find that they are more free (and awake!) at lunchtime. There are lots of good Bible reading aids, but they must be servants not masters. Another excellent way of exposing yourself to scripture may be, as already suggested, to listen to it on cassette.

Encourage organisational use

It is not enough to begin a church business meeting with a verse or two of the Bible, only to close it quickly and get on with the real purpose of the evening! Take a little time to allow its message to sink in. The Bible must be significant in the 'business' of the church as well as its worship. Keeping the Bible open in a prominent place is a useful visual reminder of this. It is important to make it clear that the principles and priorities being followed during the evening are derived from the Bible.

Our children's and young people's work, as well as ongoing work among adults, must give a high priority to the word. Each group in the church must be encouraged to find fresh and relevant ways to use the Bible and to stimulate its members to use it.

Encourage ministry use

Encourage people to bring their Bibles to church and to keep a copy in their desk at work. Suggest that it can be used to respond to a question or to stimulate discussion: 'You'll never guess what verse our minister preached on yesterday!' Many people who are not Christians will be drawn into discussion and will come back with all sorts of questions related to half-remembered stories from school: 'Doesn't it say in the Bible that . . ?' is a common query.

In counselling, try to avoid just giving good advice. Wherever possible, refer people back to verses and passages from which they can draw strength – and can continue to do so after they have left you. In general pastoral visiting, the reading of a short piece of scripture can add authority to the 'prayer before we leave'. In marriage preparation and baptismal classes, Bible passages can be used to provide guidance and strength while clearly identifying Christian forms of behaviour. Too often these classes can degenerate into focusing exclusively on where the bride's mother should sit or what the temperature of the water should be!

In all these ways we are attempting to let God's word loose among God's people. We must put into practice what we say we believe about the Bible – that it is central to our Christian life and faith.

The Bible awaits us. It is milk for the newborn Christian and meat for the mature, a feast of good things to satisfy every palate and nourish every soul. And it is food to be shared with a starving world. We have a message of invitation to the feast. The message must be proclaimed by preachers who can relate to God and modern people, and by churches absorbed in the Book of life.

> 'Gird each one with the Spirit's sword,
> The sword of Thine own deathless word;
> And make them conquerors, conquering Lord,
> Where Thou Thyself wilt come.'
>
> *Mary Gates*

8

Small Groups in the Church

THE ISSUES

When I was a child, I was what my mother euphemistically called 'well-covered'. In the words of my peers at school, I was less pleasantly called 'fatso'. My grown-up children tell me that, now I have reached the dignity of middle age, I need to beware of creeping middle-age spread. It's a battle!

But the battle reminds me that small is beautiful on two counts. I certainly feel a lot better if I am not grossly over-weight, and I have to admit it is worth the effort. Also, it takes my mind back to those pre-teenage years when belonging and being accepted was so important for my self-esteem. To be called 'fatso' in such a disparaging way, did not help in that particular exercise. So when the opportunity came to join a gang, I jumped at it. I can clearly remember the name of the gang leader (whom I did not especially like), and the promise I was able to extract from him that I would never be called 'fatso' by him or other members of the gang! All this may seem trivial but the fact that the details are so clearly etched into my mind, some forty years after the event, indicate that it was not so for me!

The need to belong

The sense of need to belong and to be accepted, is surely reflected by most, if not all, human beings if they are prepared to admit it. Even the classic 'loner' has often developed those characteristic traits precisely because he has at some stage not been accepted for what he is, but has been ostracised or rejected.

'Fellowship' must be one of the most overused and under-practised clichés in the church today. If we want to close our church in a decade all we need to do is to ensure that the idea of 'fellowship' remains simply an idea, and is not put into practice. We all know we ought to be experiencing it, and showing it, but sadly feel deprived of it in the very place that ought to be giving a lead. In his book, *The Christian Agnostic*, Dr Leslie Weatherhead observes:

> 'My faith in the Church is not faith in the drab and unbeautiful building at the corner of the road, where Mrs Smith won't speak to Mrs Brown because she was snubbed twenty years ago, or where Mr Jones resigns once a month in the hope of getting his own way and blackmailing his minister, or where Mr Robinson sings heartily that he is 'washed in the blood of the Lamb' but would not tolerate a stranger in his pew and has not paid his milkman's bills, where Mrs Jackson attends every service and adores 'our dear vicar' but makes a hell of her own home by her temper, tears and tantrums, or where committees wrangle and fight about trivialities, and gossip behind one another's backs and show less goodwill and good fellowship than one finds in a golf club committee or in any army mess where nothing is professed save decency and gentlemanliness.' (Quoted in *The Wit of the Church*, Michael Bateman and Shirley Stenning. Leslie Frewin Publishers, 1967.)

How many times have we heard – or had it happen to us – that someone has gone to a church, desperately lonely, longing to belong, only to receive not a word of welcome nor even be noticed apart from being handed the books for the service and being passed the collection plate? The regularity of such experiences only goes to show that church is, and must always be, much more than just the hour on Sundays where the people of God gather together for worship.

We all begin life in a small group. It is called 'family' and however small it may be – and it may well be just mother and child – there is a relationship of caring and nurture, and a person or people with whom there is security and trust. As human beings we have an innate need to know and be known, to love and be loved. As we grow, such small groups proliferate: Brownies, Cubs and Guides; sports teams; Christian groups; clubs of various kinds, professional groups and other gatherings of common interest. As God the Creator made us to be social beings, it should be no surprise that we work best that way, and that small groups are, generally speaking, a most effective means to that end.

Of course, because of our individualism and alienation from each other, small groups can also be terribly threatening. We fear the prospect of being known by others. Generally, we assume they won't like us if they know what we're really like! Some Christians, having had a bad experience of a small group run insensitively, have been left only with fears: a fear of *having* to reveal their inner selves to others; fear of being made to look inadequate by being asked to read unfamiliar passages from the Bible and from places that are impossible to find; fear of being put on the spot by being asked to pray aloud. Such a threatening scenario would make many Christians run a metaphorical mile. But once this barrier of fear or feeling of threat is overcome, people discover, to their amazement, a liberating sense of pleasure in getting to know others and in being known, often for the very first time.

Biblical precedent for small groups

The idea of dividing a large number of people into small groups is not new! There are precedents for it in both Old and New Testaments.

As we saw in chapter 4, right back in Exodus, Moses' father-in-law saw the need for delegation in leadership in order to provide pastoral care for the children of Israel (Exodus 18:17–23). The basic group appears to have been ten in number with leaders of tens, leaders of hundreds and leaders of thousands. This gave everyone a sense of well-being and belonging and meant that Moses himself only had to deal with the worst of the crises rather than all the everyday problems.

In the New Testament it is significant that Jesus spent the

vast majority of his time not with large groups but with twelve carefully chosen men. In this way he could guarantee the continuation of his message – these people would be able to teach others the principles that Jesus had taught them.

From the Acts of the Apostles we have further evidence of small groups in action:

> 'They devoted themselves to the apostle's teaching and to the fellowship, to the breaking of bread and to prayer. Everyone was filled with awe, and many wonders and miraculous signs were done by the apostles. All the believers were together and had everything in common. Selling their possessions and goods, they gave to anyone as he had need. Every day they continued to meet together in the temple courts. They broke bread in their homes and ate together with glad and sincere hearts, praising God and enjoying the favour of all the people. And the Lord added to their number daily those who were being saved' (Acts 2:42–27).

The believers met together in the temple courts and in one another's homes. The whole fabric of the New Testament church was geared to a mixture of large group celebration and small group fellowship, discussion and prayer. This pattern was continued for the next 200 years until distinctively 'Christian' buildings began to be built. This tandem of congregational celebration and house groups was amazingly successful: there were daily conversions, everyone's material needs were met and outsiders looking on were deeply impressed by the believers' special quality of life.

The purpose of small groups

In *Good things come in small groups* (London: Scripture Union, 1987), Ron Nicholas suggests there are four ingredients essential for vibrant Christian life: nurture, worship, community and mission. Each of these is most effectively fostered within the context of a small group.

Nurture
The early believers 'devoted themselves to the apostles' teach-

ing'. Like the Bereans, who 'examined the Scriptures every day to see if what Paul said was true' (Acts 17:11), their nurture came largely from studying the Scriptures together. Such groups can, and perhaps should, be the lifeblood of a church. Wesley certainly saw their value, as has Methodism since his time. When groups meet together just for the sake of meeting, or merely to accept the minutes of the last meeting and then to launch into a round of unmitigated gossip, one wonders about their value to the church's life. In one church we know, the new minister and his wife arrived convinced of the spiritual value of small groups. There was a women's group that met monthly and the minister's wife was invited to attend – and to lead the first meeting. She did so, beginning proceedings with a short, devotional Bible study. At the end of the meeting, a small deputation approached her, thanking her for being there and, to her consternation hoping 'that there would not be too much religion in future meetings'. But that women's group gradually changed its nature and saw new life develop – although some of the 'old school' were never really happy with the patent spirituality that came to mark its existence.

Teaching can come from a Sunday sermon, but true nurture needs the opportunity for questioning and discussion that small groups can provide. Small groups give opportunities to share at a personal level in a way that larger meetings tend to discourage. Alcoholics Anonymous learned that secret, using regular, small, sharing groups as the means of return to sobriety for countless thousands of alcoholics. In various inner-city church crypts in England, such groups show the acceptance and fellow feeling that the church itself, in its regular services, so often fails to do. Nurture is nice, and small is beautiful where most individuals are concerned. And sharing is often the cause of praise, where group members experience, through others, God working in wonderful ways. Mutual support becomes a comforting and strengthening means of growth, and the early believers knew it well.

Worship
More often than not, 'worship' brings to mind the whole congregation, lustily singing some well-known hymn or

chorus, probably with overhead projector and accompanying music group. Worship means so much more than that, and can enrich small group life when properly understood and practised.

Focusing on God, and giving God 'worth', honour and praise, can be achieved in a wide variety of ways: silence, meditation, sharing a word of Scripture or testimony, using a leaf, a candle or a picture to focus the spirit and mind on Christ and our relationship with him. The opportunities for helpful experiment are endless and the initial embarrassment some may experience from being a small group can be gently dismantled.

Community

The community ingredient is closely related to both nurture and worship. It is difficult, if not impossible, to be nurtured on God's word and to worship God, without then caring for God's people. The first Christians 'had everything in common' and no one was left in need. How different a picture is painted in our contemporary society! According to all reports, the rich are getting richer and the poor are getting poorer. In small, caring groups, needs can be shared much more easily than in large, impersonal congregations. In the former, trust has been established; in the latter, to publicly share needs would be painfully embarrassing. The Mormons

'Hancock shares the mission report, Baxter shares the financial report, Thompson shares the building report, and you share the visitation report. What do you mean there's no intimate sharing in our board meetings?'

seem to have set a shining example of caring for members of their own community, with Mennonites, Jehovah's Witnesses and Seventh Day Adventists doing similarly. Without in any way wanting to lump these groups together doctrinally, all have developed a worthy sense of community, largely through networks of small groups. Different from secular groups, Christian community is intended to be marked by love, commitment and freely accepted obligations such as we have to our family.

But the building of community is not meant simply to make life more comfortable for its members. Christian communities are always to be open to others – outward looking, mission oriented, service motivated.

Mission

One of the most effective small groups I have ever shared in was one we called Agnostics Anonymous. It was not an original name, but it gradually came to be known by that even less original name of the Enquirers' Group. There were no rules, except that no question was too stupid to be asked. We all realised that if one of us had a question on our minds, the likelihood was that it would be puzzling most of the others in the group too! A fascinating cross-section of people came, and the discussions were always stimulating, often quite fiery, and regularly frank.

Although the group had its 'floaters' who came and went, it developed a marvellous sense of belonging, and cerebral discussions often developed into pastorally sensitive sessions of caring and support.

One consistent attender was Martin (not his real name), a man who had a constant stream of questions. Many of them were 'favourite' red herrings but all were treated seriously and with respect. One evening Martin was off on his regular routine of red herrings. I felt it was time for me to act as devil's advocate, and as the discussion focused on what it meant to 'become a Christian', I suggested that Martin play the role of the pastor, while I became the enquirer.

Step by step, he took me through the stages of becoming a believer – looking at the nature of God, man's freedom, his rebellion, the consequences, God's solution, the meaning of the Cross, and the call to commitment. His explanations were impeccable. So much so that, at a perfectly appropriate time, another member of the group asked ingenuously: 'Martin, is there anything stopping *you* becoming a Christian now?' After a pause, and with a look of mischievous good humour that belied the seriousness of the transaction that was about to take place, he replied: 'No, I guess there isn't, is there?'

A means to growth

The value and importance of small groups engaged in nurture, worship, community building and mission cannot be ignored. They are the hallmark of churches that are growing numerically and individuals who are growing spiritually. Small groups are more obviously present at times of great revival, such as the Reformation in the 1500s and the birth of the Pentecostal movement in the late 1800s. Nowhere is the small group seen better than in the birth of Methodism. John Wesley's constitutional class meetings conserved the first fruits of his evangelism by gathering the new converts into small groups for Bible study and prayer. These groups met on a weekly basis and enabled new Christians (many of them illiterate and ignorant) to discuss their faith with a group leader who was more mature spiritually than they were. These groups played a major part in keeping the impetus of the Wesleyan revival going and ensuring that new Christians grew in the faith and became strong.

Whether church membership is numbered in the hundreds of thousands (as in Korea), or on the fingers of two hands, the basic principles still apply. People in general *need* what small groups offer in order to grow in faith and so to bring others into the fellowship of the church. Howard Snyder, in his book, *The Problem of Wineskins* (Leicester: IVP, 1975), highlights a number of advantages of the small group within the church, which make it a vital growth point:

• It is *flexible*. Its purpose, content and membership can change, and it might be decided in advance to limit its life span.

- It is *mobile*. It is not restricted by a building, and can meet virtually anywhere.
- It is *inclusive*. It excludes no one, and everyone is important, being noticed and missed if they don't come. How often does that happen in church?
- It is *personal*. Personal needs of members become the focus of concern, prayer and support. Mutuality, and involvement in each others' lives, becomes increasingly vital to its members.
- It is *risky*. Vulnerability is the price to pay for membership, with accountability, conflict and confrontation often proving to be the unexpected means of grace and growth. But taking risks is always an adventure!

While I am writing this, I am also involved, as a team member, in a holiday activity for over fifty eleven to fourteen year olds. They arrived in various stages of dread, anxiety, excitement, anticipation and enthusiasm. Each was placed in a small group of six or so, and the transformation in them has to be seen to be believed! They have discovered that their problems, doubts, fears and hopes are shared almost universally by all the others – they now *belong*. And the same applied to the team members, too. The discovery that not only do we need each other, but that we can each contribute to each other's security and growth, can transform both our attitudes and our inner life. A word of encouragement, a helping hand, a request for support, can all be part of 'bearing each other's burden, and so fulfilling the law of Christ' (Galatians 6:2).

THE WAY FORWARD

Very few church leaders need to be convinced of the value of small groups – in theory! So why are they such a pain in practice? Why does it never work as well in a local church as it sounded when they explained it at the conference?! Part of the answer is that people are much more difficult to organise than names on a piece of paper. In addition we also need to recognise that house groups don't just happen. In fact, for the first few months they don't solve problems in the church – they cause them; and if we don't set them up correctly they go on causing problems for a long time. It would not be an exaggeration to say that some churches have instituted small groups and regretted it ever since! Their house groups have produced disunity and division while declining numbers have seen disillusionment set in and groups disband.

Many churches would benefit from a radical rethink of their house groups, or a thoroughly biblical, helpful idea will continue to see its amazing potential unfulfilled. From time to time we need to go back to basics and examine the factors that make small group structures so vital.

House groups: the choices

There are basically five possible ways of dividing a church into small groups:

• *By geography*: Linking people together by virtue of where they live. Those churches who follow this system generally work towards a specific goal, such as setting up a group in every street, or establishing a group for every twenty-five houses in your community. (These are ideals – I don't know of any local church which has achieved either, yet!)

• *By age*: banding people together by virtue of age – groups for teenagers, young marrieds, the middle-aged, etc. This system is used by many southern Baptists in America.

• *By 'mix'*: putting folk together in order to achieve a 'mini-church' feel. It is a deliberate attempt to mix old and young, new Christians and mature, singles and marrieds, etc.

• *By subject*: giving people the choice of various study options, eg prayer, the second coming, the book of James, etc. People can work together on a subject that really captures their interest.

• *By ministry*: linking individuals with similar gifts or tasks in the life of the church – the music group, evangelism team, deacons, etc. These groups can be used for planning *and* worship.

Almost all other systems are variations on these five. Churches will decide which is most appropriate depending on their ethos and priorities. I have become committed to the 'geographical' option. I think that it adequately reflects biblical principles, makes pastoral care easier, enables attendance without transport and encourages evangelism. It also seems to make community involvement easier and provides a healthy base from which to plant a congregation in a particular area, as the church grows.

Needless to say, all the options have strengths and weaknesses. Each fellowship will have to come to its own prayerfully considered conclusions.

House groups: the leaders

Good leadership is critical if small groups are to work well. House group leaders are frontline troops: they need training, equipping and supporting, and healing when they get injured. All this must be provided, not simply prior to them becoming house group leaders, but also *during* the period of their leadership. Books, cassettes and magazine articles can be made available on most aspects of small group leadership – encourage your leaders to take advantage of them. Arrange a couple of training days each year and plan to bring in an 'expert' to supplement the expertise available locally. Don't 'molly-coddle' them but do make it clear that loving support is available if they need it.

Give guidelines for leadership

Group leaders need clear guidelines for how to lead the group. These ought to be relatively brief but demanding enough to provoke serious commitment. I use guidelines like those listed below. Group leaders will need to be taken through these guidelines to explain why each element is significant for the health of their group and the body as a whole. The list will need to be adapted to suit local variations in emphasis, but it provides a sound base from which leaders can operate.

Guidelines for group leaders

1 The purpose of a small group is to enable *each* member to be involved in the group's activity, whether this is discussion, reflection on Scripture, reading Scripture, praying, singing, or whatever else is specified as the group's aim. So please resist the temptation to use the evening as *your* opportunity to give a lecture or a talk!

2 It is important that the church family as a whole is studying similar material at the same time, so that we all move ahead together and in the same direction! This material will be provided for you. Please do not substitute your own material for this.

3 Please do not cancel a meeting or change the night on which you meet, without talking to the church leaders first. A request from the group to cancel the meeting may signify a problem that needs further exploration, and a rescheduling of a meeting may result in a clash with something else of importance to the members. Hence the need for consultation.

4 The church leaders are always available to give any help you need. Please do not hesitate to ask them for this – they are not mind-readers! It is always better to discuss a problem as it arises rather than wait until it has developed into a full-blown disaster!

5 Encourage (urge, entreat, plead with!) the members of your house group to attend whole-church gatherings for prayer and the services on Sundays. This will help the members see themselves as part of a wider fellowship, with the house group being an important, though not exclusive, part of the whole. Please model this by being faithful to these things yourself.

6 Encourage the church members in your group to give apologies when they cannot be present at the business meetings of the church. This will encourage responsible membership and the treating of others with respect.

7 Please give out to your group the notices on the sheet which the church leaders provide. They serve to keep the fellowship informed of what is happening.

8 Adopt a positive tone and attitude at all times with group members, but especially when the group meets. This will make the group easier to lead and will help develop an atmosphere conducive to praise, ministry and study.

9 Keep an upward and outward focus. Avoid letting the group become introspective, focusing merely on its own needs. It is easy to lose sight of the fact that we are called to minister to those who do not yet know the Lord.

10 Do your best to keep fresh spiritually. Often a group rises to the level of its leadership – our 'freshness' will revitalise them.

11 Do not let the group get into a rut. Always be thinking of creative ways to keep your house group meetings entertaining, exciting and meaningful. Bored group members will stop coming!

12 If you have problem attenders, please talk to someone in leadership; we would like to help you in any way we can as you encourage them to attend.

13 Please fill in the House Group Leader's Report form after each group meeting, and give it to one of the church leaders as soon after the house group as possible. This will keep us all up-to-date on news and will help us to help you quickly and efficiently.

14 Please make sure that the formal part of the house group evening is over by 9.30pm. Some people will have babysitters, etc to relieve and will not want to keep them waiting. It is easier to get everything into the allotted time if you also start promptly!

15 Please do not think the above requests are for everybody else but not you!!

Get feedback from leaders

The health of the group will need to be reviewed regularly and the way leaders are coping will need to be monitored. Without this, the guidelines will remain like an estate agent's description of a house – stimulating and exciting but bearing only passing resemblance to the facts!

One of the simplest ways to help the leader of a small group communicate back to the church leaders on how the group is doing is by providing him or her with a brief report sheet. Factual information can be passed on, pastoral needs shared, struggles in getting the information across communicated, and any concerns, grievances or joys of group members that should be shared with the leaders, passed on to them. I suggest something like the following, set out on a sheet of A4:

House Group Leader's Report

Name of leader:

Date of meeting:

Number in attendance:

What was the best thing about the evening?

Why do you think this was?

Was there any part of the evening that went badly?

Why do you think this was?

Is there anything any member of the group would like raised with the leadership?

Any other comments?

Please complete as much of this form as you feel is appropriate after each of your meetings. Please then return the form to a leader as soon as possible after the meeting, and not later than the following Sunday.

Of course, leaders of the church must treat this information confidentially and *respond* to it. And this report form must supplement personal contact, not replace it. There is no substitute for *personal* support and encouragement.

House groups: the members

The Church family must be encouraged to play its part in making the small group structure work. If people are not committed to them, their benefits will be minimal. Leaders can spell out what kind of commitment is necessary to get the best out of house groups. This can be done in sermons, bible studies, letters to the congregation or even by producing a 'Guidelines for membership' sheet which members can study. This membership sheet could contain suggestions such as these:

Guidelines for membership

- **Be there!** Try to commit yourself to attending your house group regularly. If you do so, you will soon find that you are benefitting from the warm, personal fellowship that comes with week-by-week participation in Bible study, worship, witnessing, ministering, and social activities. Your attendance and enthusiasm will encourage the other group members. Arrive on time and enjoy every moment!

  It is also important to commit yourself to attending – with the others in your house group – the weekly worship services of the church. You will find that these times of prayer, worship and proclamation of God's word will help you grow spiritually, not just on your own but alongside the others in your group.

- **Study your Bible!** Make Bible study a priority. Read your Bible daily, asking God to speak to you through it. Before the house group meets, study the passage that the group will be looking at. Take your Bible; take part in discussion; ask questions about anything you do not understand.

- **Be a friend!** Try to keep in touch with others in your group between meetings, particularly those whose interest is lagging or who are facing particular pressures or problems.

  Begin to look around in your local community for those who are not related to any church, and invite them to the house group. Introduce them to others and make them feel welcome. Minister to others in need.

- **Participate!** A house group doesn't work if it is full of spectators! Come ready to contribute in some way – to pray, worship, laugh or make a cup of tea!

  Encourage your leaders, even with just the occasional 'thank you' for all they put into the house group.

Small groups are important in small churches, and their significance increases with church size. Rightly understood and implemented they are not *a feature* of the church, they are the *heart* of the church. It is here that the doctrines of fellowship, worship and evangelism find practical expression, and where love and friendship may not only be spoken of but also experienced.

> 'Blest be the tie that binds
> Our hearts in Christian love;

The fellowship of kindred minds
Is like to that above.

We share our mutual woes,
Our mutual burdens bear,
And often for each other flows
The sympathising tear.'
John Fawcett

9

Training in the Church

THE ISSUES

Jenny was fourteen and had just been confirmed in her village's Anglican Church. The visit of the bishop had been a memorable occasion for her and her family, and for Rebecca, Jenny's schoolfriend who had persuaded her to join the confirmation class so they could do it together. They had each gone to Sunday School when they were younger and, after a few years' break, thought it would be good to get confirmed. They enjoyed the classes, and the couple who took them were good fun. In fact, they not only learnt more about God, the Bible, the church and themselves during the course, they each came to a real faith in Jesus.

When it was all over, they both genuinely felt that they would like to 'do something for God'. They noticed in the church's weekly news sheet that there was a need for Sunday School teachers for seven and eight year olds, so they offered their help to the minister. Their offer was gladly accepted and, within the month, they had begun – learning by trial and error, unaware of their awesome responsibility in communicating biblical truth to impressionable youngsters in their formative years.

Do we need training?

Perhaps this case study seems an unfortunate caricature of reality but it is, sadly, all too typical of what does happen in churches up and down the land. Lay ministry is at last being seen to be biblical, and also pragmatically necessary – sharing the load with the harassed and overworked ordained, full-time minister.

A glance at the weekly news sheet of most local churches will show a dazzling array of activities, the extent sometimes dramatically disproportionate to the size of the church and congregation. Members are rushed off their feet, loyally attempting to support their church, while leaders remain at a premium. So lay ministry proliferates, and rightly so, but training for the job is rare.

Should Jenny and Rebecca *really* have been let loose on their poor, unsuspecting, impressionable seven and eight year olds, without either skills or training or even an apprentice-ship period? Was it right to have assumed that the Holy Spirit would equip them instantaneously and miraculously with the teaching skills and psychological insights they needed? Some people may argue that such skills are unnecessary in Christian work anyway – a knowledge of the Bible and being filled with the Holy Spirit is enough, they may say.

Paul's second letter to Timothy should perhaps lead us to a different conclusion. This letter is full of practical advice, recommendations and 'skills training'. Paul doesn't urge Timothy *only* to understand the Scriptures thoroughly; in order for that knowledge of the Scriptures to be put to great effect Paul also has no hesitation in teaching Timothy how to tackle the practical problems and sticky situations that he will encounter in his ministry: 'Keep reminding them . . . warn them . . . pursue righteousness, faith, love and peace . . . don't have anything to do with . . . the Lord's servant must . . . be able to teach . . . must gently instruct . . .' and so on. What for us is now Scripture was once for Timothy skills training!

Paul knew that the work of ministering in Christ's name was so demanding that Timothy needed all the skills he could acquire. He had to be 'thoroughly equipped'. If the worlds of business and commerce, sport and academia, trades and the arts, are all aware of how important it is to be 'thoroughly equipped', how much more should the church be concerned to equip its members for the work to which God has called them! In Timothy's case, of course, that equipping came primarily from knowing the Scriptures, because the task he had been given was to teach them to others. But he also needed to learn how to communicate effectively, how to teach and how to motivate his congregation to learn!

The principle of giving training for a task is itself modelled by Scripture:

> 'All Scripture is God-breathed and is useful for teaching, rebuking, correcting and training in righteousness, so that the man of God many be thoroughly equipped for every good work' (2 Timothy 3:16).

If the church continues to drag its feet in the provision of training for its members, by the end of the decade there may be no potential leaders or workers around to train!

If it were possible, I would incorporate in full in this chapter Anton Baumohl's superb practical guide to training in the local church, *Grow Your Own Leaders* (London: Scripture Union, 1987). It should be required reading for all who wish to take training seriously. He defines training simply as, 'those activities that help equip people to carry out a particular task or take on some specific responsibility' (*Grow Your Own Leaders*, p 33).

Thinking back to local churches where we have ministered, the list of possible trainees is a long one – as many as there are tasks to be done: administrators, Bible study group leaders, bookstall organisers, care and counsel groups, a catering team, church cleaners, committee chairpersons and members, crêche workers, dance and drama teams, an evangelism group, a family service team, flower arrangers, healing ministry team, hospital visitors, a maintenance team, marriage preparation leaders, mother and toddler group leaders, the music group, news sheet editor, prayer group leaders, preachers, readers, teachers, welcomers, worship leaders, youth workers. The scope is enormous!

What we do and who we are

Even when training is taken seriously, things can still go wrong if we concentrate on teaching people only how to *do* things and do not help them to *become* the sort of people who will use that knowledge effectively. Going back to Paul's second letter to Timothy, we can see this blend of training in how to do the task in hand, and encouragement to mature into the sort of person who reflects the character of Jesus and who will go about the task in a Christlike way.

We once had a faithful group of hospital visitors which met each Tuesday for Bible study, a time of prayer, and some skills training using case studies. At the first meeting some basic skills were taught, amongst which was sensitivity, especially to patients who were very ill. Then we all left to 'blitz' the local hospital, resplendent with our official hospital name tags. Later that afternoon, the Matron rang, her voice betraying considerable strength of emotion. She told me that one of our visitors, at the bedside of a dying woman, had said: 'My, you look poorly! You look as though you could be dying!' It didn't surprise me to hear that the Matron would not welcome that particular visitor back again, and that our whole visiting programme was temporarily in jeopardy. The best of training – and, of course, I felt ours was! – is never fool proof.

This illustrates the predicament some Christians feel they are in with regard to training in the church. On the one hand, the need for trained workers is obvious. But on the other, talk of 'sensitivity' and 'awareness' smacks of the kind of self-centred humanism about which the church has been warned, the more so in recent days with the infiltration of New Age thinking into every part of life. And yet it was one person's lack of sensitivity and awareness that made that hospital visit such a disaster.

The temptation, when confronted with the need for workers and for training, is for churches to feel that training is only about 'doing', and so they neglect the 'being' aspect of those they train. It has been said that God is more concerned with who we *are*, and with our relationship with him, than with what we *do*. If that is so, we would rarely know it, judging by the hyperactivity of most church programmes. Training has to do both with 'doing' and with 'being' – with the skills required to *do* the task better; and with the 'sensitivity' and 'awareness' to *be* the kind of person who can serve another in a way that honours both God and that person.

Once trainees are aware of their need to be developing spiritually, maturing in their relationship to God at the same time as they develop practical skills, they will also become more sensitive to the needs of others. Their ministry will combine the use of *chronos* time and *kairos* time – the former being that aspect of time dictated by filofaxes, personal organisers, diaries and the clock; the latter being those events and opportunities, often unexpected, in which people take first priority.

A biblical model of training

In a day that knew nothing of marketing and management, nor of the computerised technology of the industrial training scene, Jesus demonstrated what Paul was to mean later by 'thoroughly equipping God's people for every good work'.

To start with, it involved the selection process. By even the most rudimentary twentieth-century standards, Jesus did seem to select a most unprepossessing bunch as his raw material for such a gigantic task as founding a church that was to last for ever. But by the very act of choosing those he did – even down to including the treacherous dud, Judas Iscariot – he showed how important it is to see the *potential* in people. Indeed, some might even regard that ability to spot potential as a gift of spiritual discernment.

Having selected the disciples, Jesus then invested an enormous amount of himself in their lives, abdicating the normal human comforts (let alone the extraordinary celestial ones!) to spend three solid years with them to ensure that they were thoroughly equipped. It was no light task Jesus was taking on, and if the church is to take training seriously, it will not be 'one-off shots', but a demanding, on-going commitment.

In that amazingly brief, but stupendously effective, three-year training course, Jesus incorporated three fundamental components:

1 Teaching
He was a brilliant teacher, using all the principles professional educationalists have theorised about down through the years.

He began where his learners were. He understood and related to their situation, and applied his earthy illustrations to them in a way that was intensely relevant. He used questions. He retained their attention. He fostered their curiosity. He acknowledged, and made positive use of, his hearers' emotions – their fears, joys, humour. He confronted them with choices, decisions, and the need to act in response.

And yet he respected their dignity and ensured their freedom to accept or reject his message. His teaching methods were timeless. But he was more than a teacher. He was a trainer too.

2 Modelling

In providing his own example, or model, to the disciples, he developed what has come to be called an *apprenticeship system*. Scripture Union evangelists, schools workers and trainers have a network of volunteer associates who contract in at different levels to work alongside the 'professional', observing how she does it, learning gradually by working alongside, and ultimately 'flying solo'.

3 Doing

Some may disagree, but I would contend that a trainer should not train another to do something the trainer is not already doing (or at least has done) herself. The old adage, 'if you can, do; if you can't, teach' diminishes credibility to say the least, and this should not be so in the church.

When I first taught in school, my timetable had me spending the bulk of my classroom time teaching a subject for which I had no tertiary qualifications at all. When I shared this concern with my Headmaster, his dry rejoinder was: 'Cohen, the best way to learn how to teach is to teach. Go and do it, and don't complain!' I certainly learnt a lot about that subject by taking his advice, but I always felt a bit of a fraud, struggling to keep one lesson ahead of the class.

Not so with Jesus, nor his disciples. By his teaching, modelling and doing he was training his trainers, so that the seventy were then able to go out on their first ministry tour, basically but thoroughly equipped to fulfill their calling (Luke 10:1–20).

Growth through training

The twelve and the seventy were given skills training, but it was far more than that, too. It had to do with discipleship, with being, with spiritual growth – and that is the bonus for churches that take it seriously. Ministers know what rich blessing they derive from preparation times in their own ministry, whether it be preparing sermons, Bible studies, quiet days or retreats. Why then deprive the flock of similar blessing, by neglecting the fundamental calling of the church to equip the saints?

In *Grow Your Own Leaders*, Anton Baumohl points out that the process of training people for work and responsibility in the church and community, can also:

- increase people's understanding of their ministry/service and its relationship to the church;
- fuel a vision and enthusiasm for that work
- contribute to the wholeness (health) and growth of those involved;
- be an agent of change and enable people to adapt to the changes going on around them;
- lead to the church's more effective engagement in God's mission.

There are, then, obvious advantages for the church prepared to make the costly investment involved in training.

There are also many ways of going about the task. There can be basic training, training that concentrates on problem-solving, supplementary training, and updating of thinking and skills. Training, like learning, never ends, but is part of a constant, ongoing process, for trainer and trainee alike. It can be done through books, videos and correspondence courses; through television, computers, and other audio-visual tools. These methods have been called 'distance training', and are available to churches large and small, urban or rural.

However training is done, the state of the church nation-wide makes it obvious that it needs to be done. With the church figuratively girding up its loins for a decade of evangelism, it is encouraging to see increasing evidence of training being taken seriously in some churches, dioceses and denominations. At the same time, however, we hear of highly motivated church members who, on their own initiative and often at their own expense, have gone to training courses to be of better use to the church they love, and which they want more effectively to serve. Then, back at home base, they find all kinds of barriers put in their path. An insecure or inadequate pastor, a shortsighted parish council or jealous fellow-believers – all can contribute to destroying the vast, untapped potential lying unused in the church today. Such resources need discovering, nurturing, releasing – in a word, training. It is a costly and demanding process. But the alternatives are not only unbiblical; they don't bear thinking about!

THE WAY FORWARD

Very few leaders would disagree in theory with the need for training church members but, in practice, there are often three specific obstacles that inhibit the establishment of good, ongoing, training activities.

Obstacles to training programmes

1 The fear that training is 'unspiritual'
The vitally important renewal of our commitment to the Holy Spirit's activity has led, in some cases, to an attitude of suspicion toward the apparently 'worldly' nature of training. As we have already noted, 'the Holy Spirit is all the training a Christian needs' is the (usually unspoken) base on which this attitude rests. Considering that both Jesus and Paul ran extensive training programmes which combined a reliance on the Holy Spirit with some practical teaching, it is an attitude difficult to justify.

2 Having only a short-term view
Wherever the urgent crowds out the important, training will always be low on the list of priorities. Most of us are far too busy doing the job, to have time to train others to do it. And when we do delegate, they make a mess of it, so it's obviously better to do it ourselves. Right? Wrong!

In the long-term as we have already said, it is much better to get ten people to do the work than to do the work of ten people. The leader lasts longer, the congregation feels a much greater sense of 'ownership' and belonging, and more actual work gets done! The desperate need is for local church leaders to develop a long-term mindset and be prepared for the consequences: numerical growth is likely to be slower initially, many jobs will be done less efficiently than you would like, some may accuse you of laziness and others will lose patience with the whole process! However, training of this kind will produce lasting results, if you persist.

3 The insecurity syndrome

Most leaders have areas of insecurity, not least leaders in the local church. 'What if people discover others are more gifted than me?' 'Will the congregation respect me less if others start doing certain aspects of my job better than I do?' Let's pray that both these things happen! When they do, congregations tend to respect *more* someone who recognises their own weaknesses and releases others into these areas. Many godly, gifted people in our churches are denied the training and opportunities they ought to have because of insecure leaders.

And this insecurity has a knock-on effect. Insecure leaders produce insecure followers and co-workers, constantly needing affirmation and encouragement. But this insecurity is like a black hole in space. No amount of praise, re-assurance and appreciation ever fills the 'insecurity' hole. We must find our security in God and our God-given place in his service, then others can be released to do the same.

Getting going

So, assuming we are committed to the idea of training and have worked through our reservations about it, how do we actually get it going in the local church? These four steps can form a framework for action:

1 Envision

The church family must be made aware of the needs and their responsibilities in relation to meeting them: workers are needed to maintain current ministries and to develop new ones. God's plan has always been to use leaders to train his

130

people to do the ministry – not for his people to watch the leaders do the ministry! (See Ephesians 4:11–13.) God's people need to be reminded that they are meant to be 'fellow workers' as well as worshippers (see 2 Corinthians 6:1; Romans 12:6–8). We are to be functioning parts of the body (1 Corinthians 12), as deeply committed as a soldier, athlete or farmer to the serious tasks of the kingdom (2 Timothy 2:3–6).

Perhaps a sermon series could be preached, or a series of Bible studies planned, on these passages. In as many different ways as possible the congregation needs to be alerted to their biblical responsibilities. This should provoke questions like, 'what can I do to help?' and 'what are my gifts?' as well as statements like, 'I'm no good at anything' and 'I feel God wants me to do the preaching'! Both the questions and the statements provide an excellent prod for people to realise the need for training.

One small, practical way to envision the church in this area is to publish a 'jobs list'. That is, a complete list of everything that is done in church life to keep its ministries going. The length of that list of responsibilities will normally astonish people! Add to this list things the church *should* be doing and things you would *like* it to be doing, and you have a clear indication that there is something for everyone to do! Some of the jobs can be done simply enough, but most will require an element of training. A significant minority of the jobs will require more extensive training.

2 Recruit

Asking for volunteers can be dangerous! It often results in the wrong people volunteering and can convey a sense of desperation, for example:

> '*Please* will someone volunteer to help with the under-fives; Mrs Smith had nine children *on her own* last Sunday . . . and they all cried at the same time. It's *only* an hour a week and you don't need to be *any* good with children, just willing to be there. If three or four volunteered, then you could have a rota – so you would only have to do it once a month!'

This all-too-accurate caricature denies most of what we believe in theory about ministry. It is far more effective, in the long term, to announce,

> 'Our work among the under-fives is suffering because Mrs Smith (who is doing an excellent job under the circumstances) can't cope with the numbers.
>
> We are looking for people who are willing to be trained for this vital ministry. If, having given time to prayer and reflection, you feel God may be calling you to be committed to this period of training, please let one of the leaders know. Please be open to the possibility of serving God in this significant area of church life; it will be costly in terms of time and commitment, not to mention the ear-drums! Thank you for considering this.'

There is an optional last sentence you could add: 'Until we have suitably trained staff in place, we will not be making any provision, after this Sunday, for the under-fives!' This may be a bit radical for you but I guarantee it will get the church's attention and put training at the top of quite a few people's agenda!!

It is sometimes useful to ask for volunteers on a 'just looking' basis – giving people an opportunity to ask questions about a particular ministry without feeling sucked into it before they are ready. An open evening to discuss, say, music and worship, could be organised by the worship band. Singers, musicians and those with a general interest could be encouraged to attend, as well as an invitation given to the wider church. There is no commitment, on either side, as a result of attending the evening. That is, by attending you are not offering to be committed to the music ministry nor are the music ministry committed to using you! I have found that these 'open' evenings are very well attended and also very productive in terms of producing appropriate recruits.

Leaders should not be afraid, though, of making a direct approach to people they think God might be wanting to use in particular ministries. A direct, non-manipulative, request to consider being committed to a particular task, is especially valuable for busy (often gifted) people. They may well never volunteer for anything but might be stirred into accepting a role by a fresh challenge. Besides, sometimes we are the last people to recognise our own gifts and need someone else to point them out to us.

One key principle to remember when we are trying to recruit people for training is never to minimise the work and commitment involved for the recruit. If you make it sound easy the ministry loses its value and significance to the individual. It becomes unworthy of their acceptance – 'why should I do a job that apparently anybody could do?' In addition, the 'easy approach' leads to disillusionment in the long-term, when they discover that it's not that easy after all! We would do well to emulate Sir Ernest Shackleton's advert in a London paper when he wanted recruits to accompany him on his latest exploration: 'Men wanted for hazardous journey. Small wages, bitter cold, long months of complete darkness, constant danger. Safe return doubtful. Honour and recognition in case of success.' *Thousands* responded!

3 Train

Leading in worship, teaching a children's group, running a youth group, serving communion – it all looks so easy, until you try it. Our enthusiastic recruit must be trained.

We have seen that one of the most effective methods of training was created by Jesus. We could summarise it as 'show, tell and do'. He worked miracles as a sign of the in-breaking of the kingdom, he taught his disciples the principles of the kingdom, and then he sent them out to pass on what they had seen and heard. How could we integrate these three components in training in the local church today? Let's take the leading of worship as an example. A new worship leader could attend the practices of the worship band as an observer; she could visit various churches and events and study different worship leaders at work. She could also attend seminars on worship leading, read relevant books and articles and interview some of the church leaders. As this proceeds, she could begin leading worship in the house groups, mid-week meetings and then Sunday services. All of this under the supervision of the current worship leader.

This method of training has the advantage of avoiding on the one hand the sterile, unreality of simply 'reading up'

'We're breaking in a new pianist.'

about the subject area, and overcoming on the other the bias and idiosyncrasies of a totally subjective 'thrown in at the deep end' approach. Both elements are combined in the context of 'learning by doing'.

Most local churches simply do not have the resources to provide adequate training in all the areas of expertise needed in today's church. Local leaders must be aware enough, and humble enough, to draw on the resources of the wider Christian world. These resources have never been so prolific, affordable, available and of such an excellent standard, as during this decade. (A list of helpful agencies is found at the end of this book.) It is in this area, perhaps more than any other, that the local and national agencies of the gospel can work together. It would be a dreadful waste of expertise, and to the permanent detriment of local churches, if we continue in ignorance about what is available or remain too conceited to use it!

Of course, genuine training involves the development of character as well as practical skills. A highly proficient worship leader or a superbly adept counsellor will be of limited value without the fruit of the Spirit being apparent in their lives. Paul may well have taught Timothy to preach, but he also pointed him back to Scripture itself. Paul knew that meditation on Scripture and obedience to its teaching would stand Timothy in good stead for the whole of his future ministry, because it provided 'training in righteousness'. Church leaders must pass on spiritual values through the quality of their lives as well as providing training in specific skills. Would that every 'trainer' could say with Paul, 'Whatever you have learned or received or heard from me, or seen in me – put it into practice' (Philippians 4:9)!

4 Review

Training needs to be ongoing. We ought always to be developing our skills and growing in grace. No one in the church family should be exempt from this need for performance evaluation followed by continuing training. This will keep us fresh, relevant and increasingly effective in God's work. As we submit ourselves to this process, our fellow leaders will do so more readily, and so will other workers at every level of the church family. When we review, God has the opportunity to renew.

We have a marvellous opportunity to move from merely encouraging the saints to minister, to equipping the saints for ministry. This change of emphasis must grip our churches if we are to face with confidence the challenge of being the church God wants us to be in the twenty-first century.

> 'Dismiss me not Thy service, Lord,
> But train me for Thy will;
> For even I in fields so broad
> Some duties may fulfil;
> And I will ask for no reward,
> Except to serve Thee still.'
> *Thomas Lynch*

10

A Church for the Family

THE ISSUES

The church's view of family

Sunday services are, by definition, held on Sunday, the weekly day of rest. This means that for most committed and involved believers, Sunday is anything *but* a day of rest! In fact, to combat the other endemic problem of church life, that of multitudinous meetings, some churches have decided to put all their meeting eggs into the one Sunday basket, so that at the end of the day, a typical family is utterly exhausted, needing a Monday Sabbath to recover from the so-called day of rest!

As the church seeks to serve the Christian family, it confronts a major problem. It is generally assumed in preaching programmes and church activities, that everyone lives in the supposedly ideal family group of 'mother-father-two-children-and-a-dog'. The fact of the matter is that there are more people *not* living in such a household than those who are. As a result, widowed, divorced, separated or single people and childless couples will often feel marginalised or overlooked in any structures or activities that are supposedly geared for 'the family'.

What is more, because the ideal marriage, the ideal family and the ideal home are so idealised, there is much mask-wearing in church communities, with ordinary people afraid to be honest or open, lest they be ostracised by the one group that could or should help in situations that are less than ideal. Many avoid even seeking counselling help for fear of rejection or judgmentalism.

Strangely, for all their emphasis on the importance of 'family', many churches split families up almost as soon as they step inside the doors! There is the crèche, Sunday school, Boys' Brigade, Girls' Friendly Society, Youth Fellowship, Men's Breakfast, Mothers' Union, Mums and Toddlers – and a mind-boggling variety of permutations and combinations.

Praiseworthy though it is to seek to minister to everyone in a way relevant for them, such attempts can actually disregard the family structure. In both Old and New Testaments, far more emphasis seems to be given to either the wider community family (what we might call the extended family), or to the family of faith (in the Old Testament, the people of Israel, and in the New, the church community), than to what has come to be known as the nuclear family. This is no reason, of course, to downplay the nuclear family, nor to deny its vital importance as a fundamental part of society's structure. But it does call the church to look carefully at what it is saying about 'family' by the way in which it meets together.

The church's view of children

In terms of church services, the intergenerational nature of the family presents another huge challenge and an untapped opportunity. What part do children have to play, if any? If we want to kill our churches effectively in a decade, all we have to do is to think of children as 'the church of tomorrow', and not see that they are an integral part of the church of *today*. If we do, there will surely not be a church tomorrow.

We are living with the second generation of unchurched children. What the post-war generation took for granted as common knowledge – a basic familiarity with Bible stories, biblical values and concepts – is now totally alien to most children in this country. That is why it is tragic to find faithful adults in churches who see children only as distracting and noisy, and do not think they can benefit from what the church has to offer. Again, if we do not offer them the chance to learn and to be fully integrated into the church family today, there will be no church tomorrow.

In ministering to children (or as Harding Wood put it, far more appropriately, in 'talking with children about God'), it is obviously important to have some clear aims in mind. Are we out to convert them or nurture them? As no one can be sure just when a child can come to meaningful faith, it must be both, whether we believe a child is lost until he is saved, or whether he is saved and in the family of God until he rejects that privilege.

Further, are we out to teach them facts from the Bible, using a traditional school approach, or are we aiming to model for them what it means to live in the family of God, with all that implies? Again, surely, it is both, although the 'school' approach is one that Scripture Union has moved away from in recent years. We all need facts on which to build our faith. The sad reality is that so few seem to know them these days, whether adults or children.

To serve children effectively, some radical mindshifts are still needed from those for whom the *status quo* is less threatening and more comfortable than change for the better. We like the forms of service with which we are familiar. We like to be able to retreat into a quiet, undemanding, 'reverent' atmosphere to gather our fragmented selves together again – and the presence of children who cannot conform to this threatens our security. Yet growth necessarily means change and a measure of discomfort. It sometimes means a shift in our priorities and a re-evaluation of what we consider to be most important:

> 'Then little children were brought to Jesus for him to place his hands on them and pray for them. But the disciples rebuked those who brought them.
>
> Jesus said, "Let the little children come to me, and do not hinder them for the kingdom of heaven belongs to such as these." When he had placed his hands on them, he went on from there.'   *Matthew 19:13–15*

Jesus was involved in an important ministry, and disruptive children could prevent that ministry from taking place. But the disciples had missed the point. Everyone mattered equally to Jesus; all were welcome to come and receive what was appropriate for their age or stage. Welcoming a child who loved him was as important as discussing theology with interested rabbis. We must resist the tendency to push such work to the edge of the 'real' spiritual life of the church. 'The kingdom of heaven belongs to such as these'!

But can children really come to a genuine faith? Isn't 'faith' an adult concept? There are those who genuinely believe that children are unable to come to a valid faith. Both Francis Bridger and Ron Buckland would disagree, as would Scripture Union, coming from its Children's Special Service Mission roots. (See Francis Bridger, *Children Finding Faith*, London: Scripture Union, 1987; Ron Buckland, *Children and God*, London: Scripture Union, 1986.) As I take meetings around the country, I will often ask people to raise their hands if they came to faith under, say, the age of thirteen. Without exception, there has always been a good number. By their continuing commitment to Christ, they are living testimonies to the validity of children's evangelism.

Children are part of the church family, part of the kingdom of God, and must be treated as such.

What sort of worship?

A criticism that is often raised when children are included in church worship and teaching is that the adults are deprived because of the superficiality and shallowness of the 'children's talk' approach. Yet Jesus' parables and general teaching were both simple and profound. They were able to appeal to the uneducated, and still perplex the disciples. And perhaps the 'deeper teaching' fancied by some preachers and church members panders more to their mutual pride than to their actual understanding.

At a church in Hobart in Tasmania, in the vestry before the service, the pastor said to me: 'Do be careful with the children's talk, won't you, as it's the only part of the service the adults listen to!' His wry humour may have been closer to the truth than either he or they would have been prepared to admit.

It is possible to have a balance. There is material available that can help churches function as all-age communities of faith. (See, for example, *Learning All Together*, produced by Scripture Union's *Education in Churches* department.) Such an integrated syllabus can help to keep the church family together as a whole, with both intergenerational and peer group learning and worship. Material for all-age worship and learning for adult groups, and for adult sermons, is 'all of a piece' with material for children's groups, even the under-fives. It is possible.

THE WAY FORWARD

Meetings and family life

'Meetings, Bloody Meetings' is the title of a John Cleese training video. While we may disapprove of the language, there are relatively few church leaders (or members!) who can't identify with the sentiment! Meetings on Sundays, mid-week meetings, leaders' meetings . . . and lots of children's meetings. Many parents take a daughter to a girls' group on Monday night, a son to a boys' group Tuesday night and both of them to a mixed group on Saturday night! Given the increasing pressure to take them to ballet, gymnastics and football; arrange piano lessons, teach them to swim and get involved with their school, two meetings *each evening* would not be out of the question!

Somehow, local churches must take a step back from all these meetings and analyse their effectiveness. This is particularly true in children's work because in many churches it has been such a large part of the total ministry of the church. Sadly, many churches have poured thousands of pounds and tens of thousands of hours into a children's work which is outdated, irrelevant and almost totally ineffective. And, of course, this can be true of meetings among all ages and activity-groups in the church. Far too many congregations are involved in supporting meetings which they don't enjoy, which have passed their 'sell by' date, and yet for some reason stagger on. So what can we do about all these meetings?

We need to recognise a growing cynicism in secular society

about meetings. I recently came across this poster in a busy office which sums up much of the current mood:

> ARE YOU LONELY?
> WORK ON YOUR OWN?
> HATE HAVING TO MAKE DECISIONS?
> THEN HOLD A MEETING!
> YOU CAN GET TO SEE OTHER PEOPLE,
> SLEEP IN PEACE, OFFLOAD DECISIONS,
> FEEL IMPORTANT AND IMPRESS (OR BORE)
> YOUR COLLEAGUES
> AND ALL IN WORK TIME!
> MEETINGS: THE PRACTICAL ALTERNATIVE TO WORK

Meetings in the church which simply meet the need of needing to meet will be thought of in this way! The pressure on modern family life must be eased to allow time to be together. The meetings (indeed the whole structure of meetings) of many churches began life in a totally different 'world'. This 'world' had no television, little disposable income, local employment and very limited access to transport. The 1990s provide for some high quality entertainment and information without leaving the home (video, teletext, phone, etc), one or two cars in the driveway and work up to forty miles away. Late arrival home means there's not much spare time left in the week, 'so I'm only going to go to meetings which meet a felt-need or are action-orientated'! As churches we must take these changes seriously or risk irrelevance.

Question your present practice
Once we have understood a bit more about the world our church members live in, we can begin to plan our activities. It can help to take a blank sheet of paper, try to assume you are starting from scratch, and ask yourself a number of questions. For example:

- Whose needs are we supposed to be meeting?
- What are the needs of these groups?
- Which of these needs should have priority?
- Which of these needs do we have the resources to meet

best (in terms of money, personnel, spiritual gifts, etc)?
- Which of these needs can be met by other agencies (social services, voluntary organisations and self-help groups)?
- Which of these needs can be met by other churches in the area or by the churches working together?

These questions, and others like them, are vital because they not only help to describe the task but also to limit it. No one church can accomplish everything with equal effectiveness, though many die trying! In addition, the questions help to sort out what can be done (in practice) from what ought to be done (in theory) by trying to match the perceived needs with the actual resources a church has. With restricted budgets, limited numbers of people and only a selection of the spiritual and natural gifts available, all local congregations have to choose between priorities. Questions like these help us to know how to maximise the resources we have. They also reveal areas of weakness. This will help stimulate our prayer-life as we begin to ask God to release more of his wonderful resources for these additional areas of need.

We need to be able to give clear, brief answers to the following questions about each meeting:

- Why does it take place? (What are we expecting to happen as a result?)
- What should it include (and exclude!)?
- Who is it for?
- Who is responsible for it?
- How will it be maintained and developed?

'We'll never get anywhere if you keep asking so many questions, Harry!'

If we apply these principles (and those outlined in chapter 4: 'Administration: Getting it Done') we are much more likely to have meaningful meetings which make a real impact on those who attend.

Minimise family disruption

It is possible to minimise the disruption caused to family life because of meetings. The overall number of meetings could be cut or the number of occasions people need to be away from their families could be reduced. For instance:

● Plan the church calendar in terms, giving a break from meetings between terms. This tends to provide oases of relief from pressure and ensures three 'fresh starts' a year instead of one!

● Don't have a 'three line whip' on every church meeting. Be selective. Emphasise the voluntary nature of some meetings as well as the 'mandatory' nature of others.

● Could more meetings happen on the same night? If all the children's activities happened on the same night parents would have less transporting to do, even if those activities had to be in different places. Sometimes two committee meetings can run 'back to back'. Often people prefer one night out rather than two, even if it's a long evening.

● Sometimes brief meetings can happen on the phone. A Conference Call may be quite expensive but it could save people going out. It can also focus the mind and so enable decisions to be made more quickly.

● Avoid duplication. Sometimes, for reasons lost in the mists of antiquity, very similar meetings addressing similar needs, are run in church programmes. This should be avoided.

In all this it is important to remember that attendance at meetings should not be the measure of commitment. People's *physical* presence does not *guarantee* that they are committed to Christ and his church. However, *lack* of attendance is sometimes a sign of diminishing support for the local body of believers, and their Lord. People should want to meet together with other Christians not only because it is right (see Hebrews 10:25) but also because our meetings are interesting and meaningful.

Integrating the family

The last ten years have seen an explosion in work among teenagers. This has been shown in the rapid development of parachurch organisations working among young people, the number of books being printed about working with this age group and more and more churches appointing 'youth ministers'. The 1990s will, God willing, see a continuation of these exciting ministries; but in the church as a whole, there is bound to be a change in emphasis. The teenager is becoming an 'endangered species': there are likely to be twenty-five percent fewer teenagers in this decade than in the last. Already the world's focus is switching to children and this trend is likely to continue through the decade.

All this means that our approach to children in the church is going to take on a new significance within contemporary culture. I believe we have the best chance since Robert Raikes brought learning to read and write into a Christian context, to influence society through our work with children. In order to grasp this opportunity however, we are going to have to start thinking *family*. In many churches today the largest number of meetings revolve around children alone – Sunday School, Brigades, Brownies, clubs of various kinds, even the crèche. Some churches have even emphasised children's work to the exclusion of meaningful work among adults. Treating a child as if it was totally detached from 'family' influences is a recipe for failure.

Involving parents

Any teaching by the church of children from Christian homes should be on the understanding that their parents are ultimately responsible for the children's Christian education. The couple of hours a week that the church may put in (compared with all the time spent at school and home), is best spent reinforcing the parents' efforts. Consultation and co-operation between church and parents are therefore vital.

Children from homes where there is no open expression of faith are also their parents' responsibility. This means that a relationship with these parents is also vital. As a general rule, the traditional Sunday School has failed to win these children to Christ or draw their parents to him. It could even be said that it has, in some cases, had a negative effect – inoculating these children with just enough 'religion' to prevent them ever being likely to catch the real thing!

So Christian education for children in the 1990s must think in terms of 'family'. Of course, single parents and step-parents feature increasingly in our churches and this demands sensitive and careful handling by those who have a children's ministry. Whatever kind of family the children come from, it must be involved as fully as possible. Schools are increasingly using parents in various aspects of school life, keeping them informed of their child's progress and even getting them involved in decision making as parent-governors. The church must not lag behind!

In practical terms, a number of different models are being used in churches today for integrating children into the life of the church, and for involving their parents or guardians. If your church currently operates a 'Sunday School' system, you could involve the parents in the following ways:

● Arrange parents' evenings to discuss future curriculum, style and approach to teaching, and also to give each class teacher a chance to show the work the children are doing.
● Present end of term 'reports' on each child. This could cover verses memorised, stories remembered and general attendance; it should also involve some kind of assessment of spiritual development (for example, is there any concept of 'worship' yet? Does prayer play a part in their lives? etc).
● Encourage children to sit with their parents during church. Provide some written guidelines to ensure that parents help their children get the best out of worship. Other church members could offer to sit with lone parents in church to assist with their children.
● Provide 'homework' from time to time. The follow-up material to the formal time together can reinforce the idea of partnership between parent and teacher. It also acts as a stimulus for the parent to spend some quality time with the child.

Other churches have moved away from the 'school' approach and try to create more of a family feel in the way children are taught and involved in the life of the church.

All these ideas should be supported by teaching which is thoroughly biblical, very visual, and clearly applied. It should be taught in a context where a genuine 'spirituality' is encouraged. Worship, prayer, even spiritual gifts, can all be part of a child's experience. Of course, they must not be coerced into anything, but opportunities need to be found for children to enjoy God and minister to others, at their own level. It's also helpful to have *men* as well as women leading in children's work. Those involved need to have real spiritual maturity; children's work is no place to dump fourteen-year-olds who might otherwise leave the church, or inadequate individuals who find children 'sweet'. It is a vital ministry that lays the foundation of a person's view of God and of his or her relationship to him.

Reaching non-Christian and uncommitted parents
We need to make particular efforts to reach the parents of the children in the church. The chances of our achieving anything lasting, spiritually, in these children are increased a thousand-fold if their parents also begin to get involved with the church and come to faith in Christ. So it is important that we have strategies for reaching them. We could:

• Appoint someone gifted in evangelism to be linked with the children's work. This church member could be involved (perhaps with the teacher or group leader) in visiting parents.
• Go for quality not quantity. It's better to have meaningful contact with a few uncommitted parents than to be 'baby-minding' dozens of kids so that parents can have a peaceful Sunday morning at home! Be firm about this. Those parents who are not offended will have a greater respect for the church and a deeper appreciation of its Christian education programme.
• Involve parents in 'project work'. If the children are raising money for an orphanage in Romania, or collecting tinned food for 'Help the Aged', draw on parental support. They are much more likely to be drawn to faith if they feel they are making a valuable contribution to something and meeting

Christians in a social context.

● Link each children's worker with a prayer partner in the church. Specific attention could be given to praying for the non-Christian family. This does of course, need to be done discreetly and confidentially.

All in all, our meetings for children need the same kind of serious attention all our other meetings warrant. Only then will the announcement of a meeting in our church programme be greeted with joy rather than boredom, anticipation rather than dread!

> 'Grant us wisdom so to train them
> That no mortal evil stain them;
> Young for Jesus would we gain them –
> For our children, Lord, we pray.'
>
> *Charles Pilcher*

11

Pastoral Care

'When they had finished eating, Jesus said to Simon Peter, "Simon son of John, do you truly love me more than these?"

"Yes, Lord," he said, "You know that I love you."

Jesus said, "Feed my lambs."

Again Jesus said, "Simon son of John, do you truly love me?"

He answered, "Yes, Lord, you know that I love you."

Jesus said, "Take care of my sheep."

The third time he said to him, "Simon son of John, do you love me?"

Peter was hurt because Jesus asked him the third time, "Do you love me?" He said, "Lord, you know all things; you know that I love You."

Jesus said, "Feed my sheep." '   *John 21:15–17*

THE ISSUES

Pastor or evangelist?

Feed my lambs. Take care of my sheep. Feed my sheep. Jesus left Peter in no doubt as to the importance he placed on pastoral care for the church he founded. The image of the good shepherd is one of the indelible memories of many an adult's Sunday School days. The picture of Jesus, with a lamb on his shoulders, has been a source of great comfort to innumerable struggling souls. The joy of finding the one lost sheep while the ninety-nine are left in the open country (Luke 15: 1–7) has been the inspiration of stained glass windows, paintings, hymns and choruses, reflecting the 'rejoicing in heaven over one sinner who repents.'

Semantically, the words 'shepherd' and 'pastor' mean the same, but in this parable of Jesus, the priority seems to be evangelism. All the shepherd's energies are spent in going and looking for the single lost sheep, almost at the expense of the ninety-nine who symbolise the righteous, or the saved. However, most pastors experience the opposite: the vast majority of the resources and energies of the local church are devoted to the righteous, while little is done, despite the best of intentions, for those outside the flock. Indeed, when 'outsiders' or 'incomers' happen to come along to church, and don't quite fit the monochrome nature of some congregations, they are often made to *feel* they don't quite fit, and are quickly lost again

One New York Methodist minister, however, saw the need to bring his 'ninety-nine righteous' sheep back into the fold. He put an advert in the local paper:

> 'Lost, stolen or strayed. A large flock of Methodist sheep. They have been gone for some time. When last seen they were browsing along the road of indifference. Anyone finding these sheep please bring them home, if possible, and you will receive ample reward. If they refuse to come home drive them to the nearest fold, lock the door, and report to the undersigned. Plenty of fodder will be provided on Sunday.'

Could Jesus have been telling Peter – and through Peter, the church at the latter end of the twentieth century – that pastoring and evangelism are inextricably entwined?

Pastoring for spiritual growth

Could it also be that Jesus was warning Peter – and us – that pastoring is more than sharing 'warm fuzzies' with members of the congregation to make them feel good? The passage quoted at the beginning of the chapter concludes: 'Jesus said this to indicate the kind of death by which Peter would glorify God. Then he said to him: "Follow me!" ' (John 21:19).

Pastoring was going to be a risky, costly and painful experience for Peter, and it still is, for both the pastor and the flock. This should not surprise us. After all, why does a shepherd keep sheep? Probably either to fatten them up for slaughter or to be shorn of their fleecy wool! As Christian 'sheep' our calling is to take up our cross daily and follow Jesus. Although godly pastoring will bring comfort to the bereaved, hope to the despairing, and encouragement to the pastor, it is pastoring for a purpose. Pastors are given to the church, Paul writes, 'to prepare God's people for works of service, so that the body of Christ may be built up until we all reach unity in the faith and in the knowledge of the Son of God and become mature, attaining to the whole measure of the fulness of Christ' (Ephesians 4:11–13). There is a cost involved in such spiritual growth.

The general principle is clear. Pastoring is focused on preparing the flock for maturity and wholeness, and at times this will mean 'disturbing the comfortable'. It may even be confrontational. At all times though, sensitivity and discernment are needed, as expressed by the words of the familiar prayer:

> 'Lord grant me the serenity to accept the things I cannot change; courage to change the things I can; and wisdom to know the difference.'

Pastoring is also, of course, about 'comforting the disturbed'. Within days of our returning to Mauritius after my ordination, my first two pastoral responsibilities called for depths of compassion, the likes of which I had not been forced to find before.

The first was a woman doctor who had given premature birth to a stillborn baby. She and her husband were devastated, all the more because of what was then the primitive nature of the business of funeral directing. It ended up with the husband and me having to put the tiny coffin into the back of my van, taking it to the cemetery, and carrying it to the grave for burial. Comfort was clearly called for in that case.

The second was the mother of one of our youth club members. She had been rushed to hospital with a severe heart attack, and died while I alone was with her.

So it fell to me, at the request of the medical staff, to break the news to the distressed family, including the husband who himself had a very weak heart. Both instances required pastoral sensitivity and comfort.

Caring Enough to Confront was the title of a book I later read (David Augsburger, *Caring Enough to Confront: The Love-Fight*. Ventura, California: Regal Books, 1973). I determined to put its wisdom into practice, and did so with two men for whom I had been caring for a while. I had also become involved with their families, who were being affected by their problems. For one – we'll call him Gerry – the problem was alcohol; for the other – we'll call him Rob – it was gambling. The general integrity of each was up for questioning, because of their respective problems. Could confrontation work?

Well, in one case it did and, despite a series of ups and downs, the life of the alcoholic is now on a comparatively even keel, with the marriage salvaged and strengthened. Confrontation worked, and our friendship grew. In the other case, the confrontational method was an unmitigated disaster. Our friendship was ruptured (seemingly irreparable to date), and the root problem was left unchanged.

Change has to be desired

A basic lesson Marlene and I learnt in that situation was that change has to be desired. If people do not want to be 'prepared for works of service' it cannot be enforced. And we cannot solve everybody's problems. We live in a broken, fallen world, and the church will reflect that brokenness and fallenness. All the while, its pastors need to bring into play Christ-sized quantities of love, mercy and patience.

People must be encouraged to mature

Our failure also taught us another major lesson that has stood us in good stead since. We had felt we should be unstintingly supportive to people in need, whoever they were, and whenever the need arose. Our home became like a casualty department for people who were emotionally, spiritually or physically distressed. Often, however, we were aware that a kind of 'spiritual blackmail' was being exerted on us: 'I *depend* on you spiritually, so you *must* help me.' The blackmail was more often applied to Marlene than me and it caused our own family life to suffer. We began taking a different line with such people when we realised that pastoral care meant working for the *wholeness* of the individual, to enable them to 'become mature, attaining to the whole measure of the fulness of Christ' (Ephesians 4:13).

To observe a person moving from a broken dependence, 'tossed back and forth by the waves' (Ephesians 4:14), to a growing maturity, proper self-dependence and dependence on God, was one of our great pastoral encouragements. It was especially encouraging to see such transitions become permanent. But we also discovered that this could be achieved only when two major steps had been taken by us.

● *We had to understand where the other person was coming from.* What was actually causing the crisis? In spite of all the pastoral theory I had read, understanding others only began to happen for me because of a woman we'll call Shirley. She was elderly, physically frail, with a life history of tragedy that is the stuff of which novels are made. We felt genuinely sorry for her. But that sorrow was difficult for me to express when, early on a Monday morning she rang to say that she was worried about a doctor's appointment she had to attend in three weeks' time. She wasn't sure how she would get there or what times the bus left. Monday morning – the preacher's traditional day off (although it was rarely mine!) – and three weeks ahead of the event! Couldn't she have waited?! My patience was sorely tested.

But it was stretched to the limit when she phoned late one night to tell me that her cat had disappeared. A cat? Near midnight? I don't like cats (a trait inherited from my father, I suspect), and did it *really* matter so much that she had to ring so late at night? I was about to explode when I had a road-to-Damascus type experience. It was as if God were saying to me, directly and very personally: 'David, just pause a moment and think what that cat means to Shirley. It's the only means she has to experience affection. In fact it's her life-line. Don't feel so harshly.'

It was a radical, painful but liberating lesson – one that I have been in the process of learning ever since: to understand where the other person is coming from, to try to feel what she is feeling, to walk where he is walking, as it were.

● *We had to face reality in our own lives.* And we also had to *communicate* that reality to our congregation, so they knew what we are really like as human beings!

We discovered that we had to take off the mask of pastoral perfection that many congregations put on their pastor and family, so that it becomes a 'Phantom of the Opera'-type game. Such honesty was, and is, risky. Some said we were unwise to do it, that we would lose the respect of 'our people', but we were convinced that being placed on a pedestal was of no help to anyone.

Our church weekend was the opportunity we chose. Rather than have the traditional visiting speaker, we decided as a family that we would take the sessions ourselves, entitling the weekend 'Facing Reality'. The children were in their mid-teens at the time, and were superb as they honestly, yet with sensitivity and loyalty, told of some of the problems and difficulties we had had as a family. Of course we were, and had to be, selective in what we shared. But as we shared some of the pressures we had experienced, and mistakes we had made, in our marriage and in our relationships with one another, we felt that lines of communication were thrown open. We found that people began to realise *we* could identify with at least some of the experiences *they* were going through. We felt more loved than ever, and our pastoral usefulness certainly did not diminish, but grew from then on.

We would warmly commend to all involved in pastoral ministry, that you face yourselves and your family life with integrity and honesty, and that you are not afraid to let those in your pastoral care know how things are with you. It is not easy, and we are still not fully there, but the process and the benefits are certainly worth the vulnerability, the pain and the effort involved.

'I was going to phone the police, but then I thought, "No, what they need is a pastoral call."'

Shared pastoral care

Pastoral care is another area of the church's ministry in which we have seen the need for lay involvement. It cannot be limited to the 'ordained' pastor. For example, I could not personally identify with the problems of alcohol or gambling faced by Gerry and Rob. But Gerry became a valued contact for others struggling with the same problem as him. He became a living example of hope for those feeling defeated by despair.

Similarly, in recent years we have been amazed by the

increasing incidence of child abuse among church members, by parents of whom such behaviour would never have been expected. When we cannot identify with the trauma and grief this causes, the most effective support will often be found with others who can personally identify with the problem. In just the same way, the members of 'Flying Solo' groups can provide support for others who, like them, have been widowed, bereaved, or are single or separated.

In addition to lay congregational pastoral care, a wide range of other resources are available. They ought to be tapped by the Christian pastor, whether they are overtly 'religious' or 'secular', whether 'spiritual', 'psychiatric' or 'medical'. We had a good working relationship with a local 'secular' psychiatrist. There were times when he felt he had reached the end of his tether with particular clients. Feeling he could do no more, he would refer them to us. He acknowledged the validity of spiritual, pastoral ministry. At times, we would feel out of our depth with someone we were trying to help but had confidence to refer him or her to that psychiatrist. The beneficial results were sometimes striking. Mutual confidence and sharing of pastoral care is surely to be encouraged! As someone has put it:

'Lord, grant me *courage* to do right, when doing wrong or doing nothing at all would be easier. *Wisdom* to say the right thing at the right time, because words have the power to help or hurt. *Faith* in the goodness of humanity, because living in doubt and fear is not living as you meant it to be. And most important, *love*, the kind that gives without demanding, supports without holding too tightly, and understands that we are, all of us, imperfect.'

THE WAY FORWARD

'Handling people need not be so difficult – all you need is inexhaustible patience, unfailing insight, unshakeable nervous stability, an unbreakable will, decisive judgement, infrangible physique, irrepressible spirit, plus unfeigned affection for all people – and an awful lot of experience.' (Eric Webster)

Most church leaders would agree! Pastoral care seems one of the most difficult tasks in the local church. You can't define it, yet everyone seems to want more of it and to increase its quality; some people do it without realising they are doing it and others are appointed to do it and do it badly! It's hard to know if you are doing it properly because if you do it wrong you only find out when it's too late to do anything about it. The only way you know that you are doing it right is that you are not being criticised for doing it wrong! It's a task which began yesterday, continues today and will only finish tomorrow . . . which, as we know, never comes!

Three myths

We need to establish clear principles for practical pastoral care if we are not to join the growing numbers of disillusioned and frustrated carers. Firstly, however, wrong thinking and unrealistic expectations on the part of local congregations need to be corrected. There are at·least three 'myths' that have infiltrated many fellowships, making the task of pastoral care very difficult. These issues need to be addressed in sermons, Bible studies, church magazines and business meetings.

Myth 1: The clergy are omnicompetent!
This is one of the oldest, most common myths in church life. One person cannot care for the entire flock. It is impossible to shepherd effectively more than a relatively small number of people. What's more, many congregations want not only a shepherd, but a sheep dog and vet as well – someone to chase up non-attenders and cure all the ills of anyone who has a problem! People must be helped to see that such expec-

tations are unbiblical and unrealistic. And they must be convinced in *practice* not just theory. Many a congregation who would pay lip-service to the theory still believes that a visit from anyone other than the minister is somehow second best!

Churches who seem to have solved this problem with a well-accepted plurality of leaders (and there are fewer genuine examples of this than we sometimes claim) need to beware. Clergy omnicompetence is not solved by replacing it with 'leaders' omnicompetence'. The myth is merely shared out between more people. The whole church body must be alert to the needs of others; it must be encouraged to act as a family, concerned for the well-being of the other family members. Of course, some leaders will have pastoral care as their top concern in the fellowship; they will work hard in visiting, caring and prayer ministry. But the congregation must never see this as a reason for abdicating their own pastoral care responsibility.

Myth 2: Care can be 'total'

Somehow, people have come to expect that all their needs – social, physical, emotional, spiritual – will be met by the church. 'The church can provide money if I get into debt, arrange transport when my car breaks down, plan activities to keep my little Billy out of mischief in the evenings, write me a job reference and sign my passport photograph!' Now all these things, in themselves, are perfectly legitimate parts of church life, but should not be regarded as *rights*. Such care is, rather, experienced as part of the *privilege* of belonging to God's family. Perhaps our churches are so often characterised by a lack of gratitude because we assume that pastoral care is a *right* that we should expect, rather than a *privilege* for us to enjoy.

We've probably all witnessed the painful spectacle of someone's goodwill being taken advantage of. There must be many accountants, doctors and solicitors in our fellowships who have been button-holed by other church members and expected to give free advice on a particular problem. Ways must be found to protect such people from this and to educate our congregations about abusing their relationships with other brothers and sisters in Christ.

In summary, from the perspective of leadership, pastoral care is a God-given duty and responsibility; from the perspective of the congregation, pastoral care is a privilege to be received with gratitude, not a right to be received with indifference!

Myth 3: There is a solution for every problem
Actually, this is true, but we may not experience the solution this side of heaven. Some problems are removed by God here and now, some are not. Some problems ease with the passage of time, some merely change and take different forms. As we have noted already, the aim of pastoral care is not primarily to remove problems but to produce God-dependent individuals. Jay Kesler summarises the issue:

> 'The toughest expectation facing the modern pastor is that there's an easy solution to every problem, and that the pastor ought to be able to provide it. People today don't want to hear that life is sometimes hard, that pain is a part of life, and that God may not even tell you why you're having to struggle or suffer. But people seemingly expect the pastor to make life pain free.' (Jay Kesler, *Being Holy, Being Human*. Word)

This myth must be exploded. God's grace is available in large enough quantities to support us when his power is not used to remove the problem. Miracles or release from difficulty should, of course, be asked for in faith and – if given – received with gratitude. Their absence, however, is to be received with composure and fortitude. The most skilful pastoral carer will not be able to solve all our problems.

Effective pastoral care

The pastor will find the need to provide two main types of care, and both are important: proactive and reactive.

Proactive care
Proactive care aims to tackle problems either before they arise or before they have grown to major proportions. It's motto is, 'prevention is better than cure'. Here are some areas of church life in which it can be practised:

• *Preventative measures*. It is obviously better to run thorough marriage preparation classes than to have to provide counselling after a divorce. Yet not enough churches take this aspect of pastoral care seriously. Marriage preparation classes, baptismal preparation, Bible studies on debt, special seminars for parents with babies, or on mid-life crises, etc, should all be considered carefully.

Because we are always hard-pressed in dealing with symptoms in pastoral care, we rarely stop to examine the cause. A long-term strategy of pastoral care must involve addressing some of life's major issues in advance of them being faced. You could construct a syllabus, basing the subjects on the ten most common pastoral problems you have had to deal with in the last couple of years!

• *In life's crises*. All churches need to have in place structures of support to respond to crises. Bereavement, a miscarriage, a sudden redundancy – all these issues need a prompt, personal response from someone in leadership. I have found this works best where there is a small-group system operating and house group leaders can relay such vital information to the leadership rapidly. This is especially crucial where the crisis has left people shaken and confused. Pastoral care at these times is more about simply being there than about saying anything much. A brief prayer, a hand held in silence and the offer of a cooked meal, may be the most profound contribution you could possibly make.

• *In life's major events*. A birth every half a second, a marriage every half a minute! Pretty common activities really . . . yet each single event is precious to the people involved. Too often churches have put their people through an automatic production line experience when what they really needed was a hand-crafted, one-off event. We must work hard to personalise these great moments of human experience. We may know the wedding ceremony by heart but that's no excuse for missing the heart of the wedding ceremony: love, relationship and partnership.

It has been my policy for some time now to write to members of the congregation on their birthday and on special anniversaries. I find that this simple gesture evokes more expressions of appreciation than almost any other single token of care. If it matters to them, we must make sure it matters to us! Time invested in this 'personalising' process is time wisely and productively spent.

● *Care for no reason*! Genuine love for people, and its expression in practical care, cannot be entirely expressed in a system – however sophisticated. You also need some plan by which 'unplanned' spontaneous expressions of care can be organised to happen! I don't tell my wife I love her only on her birthday or on our wedding anniversary . . . I sometimes tell her for no obvious 'reason' at all. I don't need a 'reason' – I tell her because it's true.

Genuine love will result in the occasional phone call to a church member, just to say, 'I'm praying for you' or 'thanks for all you do', or even 'how's things?' A note of appreciation or a card, can bring much affirmation to even the most mature, committed members of the church family. Keep on the lookout for ways to express support and concern.

● *Through maintaining good relationships*. The very best pastoral support flows out of good relationships. Members of our churches need to become friends! A house group leader with a dozen people to look after can work at building friendships with the group, and among the group members. This takes time – playing, praying, studying, worshipping and working together. We must encourage people to develop transparent relationships with each other, so that they can offer meaningful support to each other when all is far from 'well with my soul'!

House group leaders, in turn, need someone to offer 'pastoral care through friendship' to them. We all need someone who cares enough to love us unconditionally and offer support; as well as being enough of a friend to confront us when we stray off line. Such deep relationships should be cultivated at every level of church life.

Reactive care
It is important to recognise the limits of proactive care. If you worked twenty hours a day, every day, with twenty others doing the same thing, the pastoral task would never be finished! Inevitably, we are also going to be involved in reactive care. There is so much need in any community that

we must put a significant onus on the congregation to *ask* for the help they need rather than go along with their assumption that church leaders have the most incredible gifts of discernment. It is vital, though, that we do not 'molly-coddle' God's people; we must encourage them to develop their personal relationship with the Lord – he is the ultimate source of all strength and support. At the same time they need to know that if they need human help to supplement this, they need only ask.

- *Clarify the 'system'.* It is important that people know *how* to ask for help. Should they phone? Write you a letter? Catch you after church? Go to the home group leader first? Most congregations will not be comfortable with reactive pastoral care unless they know exactly who they should approach and how. Whatever system you devise, it should be *communicated* to people (and reviewed) regularly.
- *Provide specific opportunities.* It is sometimes helpful to provide particular opportunities for people to seek help. For example, make it known that one of the leaders is available in a private room for half an hour after each service; have a set time each week when the minister is available in his study to see people (without an appointment). Some pastors set aside a whole Saturday once every three months and invite anyone who wants to talk about anything to come for a personal conversation.

Probably one of the most significant areas of pastoral concern is that of healing. Hardly a week goes by in most churches without someone having to go in to hospital for surgery, developing a serious illness or suffering emotional distress – let alone all the usual aches and pains. I've found it useful to let people know that leaders are always prepared to pray for healing, and anoint with oil, if asked to do so. Small groups are a good place for such prayer to take place. Opportunities can be given in Sunday worship for prayer ministry with the laying on of hands – and this can be very powerful. Sometimes we need to be made more aware that God is interested in our bodies and minds as well as our spirits.

Pastoral care must be both proactive and reactive if the people of God are to be 'shepherded' adequately. Major portions of time should be set aside by local church leaders to assess the best way to carry out this task. And then, of course, a significant amount of time will be absorbed in actually *doing* the pastoral care.

Pastoring God's flock is such a significant task that there is a danger of the church and leadership becoming problem-oriented, and so weighed down, even discouraged, by this ministry. We must recognise that where there is body life there is body odour! But we must focus on the life, not the odour, so that we can continue to provide positive pastoral care to a hurting church; keeping our focus on Christ, not the problems.

> 'To watch and pray, and never faint;
> By day and night strict guard to keep
> To warn the sinner, cheer the saint,
> Nourish Thy lambs, and feed Thy sheep.'
> *James Montgomery*

12

Commitment

THE ISSUES

There are very few churches where 'commitment' is not a big issue. Casual attendance and 'fringe' involvement is relatively easy to encourage but moving people into the centre of church life, into the committed core membership, can be extremely difficult. Even the largest churches, with huge crowds on a Sunday, can find themselves supported by a fairly small group of dedicated believers. These are the people who are around when work needs to be done, attend the prayer meeting and don't drift away when the minister leaves!

The need for commitment

We are fighting a trend in society itself. As the twenty-first century approaches, loyalty, devotion to duty and reliability are not exactly stressed as vital attitudes to hold! What's more, the effect of more leisure time, better leisure facilities and increasing affluence have led to the 'weekend-away' syndrome, in addition to the traditional holiday. Television, video, concerts and many other forms of entertainment have turned us into a nation of spectators rather than participants. Fads and fashions are present in more areas of modern life; trends appear and disappear with equal ease. Permanence is rare in this world of 'built in' obsolescence. Jobs change more frequently, so people move house more often, which makes involvement in any aspect of community life (including the church) more difficult.

No wonder it is hard to engender deep loyalty to our local churches and their activities! But we must try, not only for the sake of the church, but also for the sake of those who are crying out for a sense of stability and 'belonging' in their uncertain lives.

During the final decade of this century, we need to call Christians back to a robust, determined and tenacious commitment to Christ and his church. We need to ask God to raise up an army of men and women who won't be 'seven-day wonders', who won't 'church-hop'; but who will fight and not grow weary of battle and who will have a total loyalty to their Commander-in-Chief. They are the kind of people John Wesley was looking for when he said, 'Give me one hundred preachers who fear nothing but sin and desire nothing but God, and I care not a straw whether they be clergymen or laymen, such alone will shake the gates of hell and set up the kingdom of God on earth.'

How much we need the dogged determination and godly persistence – so uncharacteristic of our age – of the missionary workers of past centuries! In West Africa it took fourteen years of missionary work before there were any conversions; in East Africa, ten; in New Zealand, nine; and in Tahiti, sixteen! William Carey worked for seven years before the Hindu, Krishna Pal, became his first convert. In Burma, Judson had to work seven years before he saw any results from his ministry. On one occasion he wrote home to say, 'Beg the churches to have patience. If a ship were here to carry me to any part of the world, I would not leave my field. Tell the brethren success is as certain as the promise of a faithful God can make it.'

Attitude to money and possessions

As local churches become more committed, money and possessions come increasingly under God's spotlight. Materialism has gripped our world and the church has not escaped the chill which its icy fingers bring. Warm, sacrificial giving is at a premium when there are so many things we *must* own, places we *must* go, experiences we *must* have and fashions we *must* keep up with. . . . all of which take our money to accomplish. So all-pervasive is this, that we hardly acknowledge that our attitudes are numb with the frost-bite of self-indulgence. Missionaries live in poverty, the mission of the church is stifled, our buildings are in disrepair or even decay. . . . not to mention the scale of hunger and homelessness with which our world is afflicted. And all while many western Christians live in relative luxury, apparently unmoved by the missed opportunities of the church and the appalling need of humanity as a whole!

If we are to be a powerful, relevant part of our society, as we rush toward the twenty-first century, we must call our churches back to a commitment which involves our resources. At the very least we can stimulate Christians to bring this part of their lives under the scrutiny of God and his word.

Tithing

'We'll give it a go, but just for one year,' the church treasurer sighed, 'and if it doesn't work (his tone of voice clearly indicated that he didn't think it would!), we'll have to go back to what we're doing now.'

The ministry of the Cohen family had just made a rather radical move. From coordinating the work of the United Bible Societies throughout the whole of the continent of Africa, I had been asked to minister in a tiny, pocket-handkerchief-sized parish in Sydney. Twenty-three people in the main morning congregation were what met the family and me as we started this new chapter of ministry together.

We had always taken tithing (giving one tenth of our income) as the norm of the Christian life, and it seemed as natural to apply that to the congregation as it did to ourselves. At that time the sum total of the church's giving outside the parish was $254, not a large sum by any calculation.

The treasurer's understandable concern was that there were not sufficient funds to cover what he considered essential items, such as the painting of the guttering on the church cottage! It was no wonder he faced with fear and trepidation the prospect of giving away a tenth of the church's income to needs outside the church, and its *gross* income at that (including the rent paid by the play group that used the church hall).

The outcome of the story is a happy one, and I believe the principle works wherever it is applied. At the end of the year, giving outside the church had multiplied tenfold to over $2700. Not only was the treasurer's pocket touched, but his heart was too. Although in his seventies, and from a church background of formal nominalism, he began to experience something of the adventure of the life of faith. Over a period of less than three years, that tiny congregation of twenty-three grew to 180 or so. The church cottage gutters were painted, and the cottage itself transformed into a centre caring for children with Downs' Syndrome. As all this happened people realised the truth of Jesus' words that it is 'more blessed to give than to receive' (Acts 20:35).

When Paul wrote his letter to the Corinthians, he reminded them that news of their generosity had spread even as far as the Macedonians. It was in that context that he taught about freewill giving, not under compulsion, 'for God loves a cheerful giver' (2 Corinthians 9:7).

The Greek word for 'cheerful' is the word from which we derive our word, 'hilarious'. Now I've had the privilege of preaching in, and attending, many churches in a lot of different countries throughout the world. And I would have to say that I have rarely seen what I could describe, by any stretch of the imagination, as hilarious giving as the plate, bag or collection dish is passed around (or even in those countries of Africa, Asia, or the Pacific where members queue up and put their offering publicly into the receptacle, overseen often by a lugubrious elder).

I used to hesitate about preaching or teaching about money and giving, feeling that 'God's work done in God's way will never lack God's provision' – the foundational principle of Hudson Taylor's work and the China Inland Mission, later to become the Overseas Missionary Fellowship. I still respect those who hold that view, but I no longer believe such a view precludes teaching a congregation about giving, nor letting the needs be known.

It was one of our co-workers who helped me shift in my understanding. He felt that, by my lack of teaching on giving and stewardship, the congregation was actually being deprived of their right to be fed the whole gospel. I had to concede the point. As I carefully prepared for my maiden attempt it was not difficult to find more than enough biblical material to expound.

Tithing is, admittedly, a predominantly Old Testament concept, but it is presented as a basic principle that would seem to hold good for all time. Even if it is a principle to which we are not held today it was the norm for the people of Israel, and could we actually justify lowering our standards as God's people of the new covenant? ' "Bring the whole tithe into the storehouse" ', Malachi had written, ' "that there may be food in my house. Test me in this," says the Lord Almighty, "and see if I will not throw open the flood gates of heaven and pour out so much blessing that you will not have room enough for it" ' (Malachi 3:10).

As I prepared my teaching material on tithing, passages like this made exciting reading, and called to mind the cottage guttering, and the treasurer, and that tiny parish. The tithe was to be on everything (Leviticus 27:30) and it was to be of the 'firstfruits' (2 Chronicles 31:5). God was not happy with the small-change mentality that seems to characterise so much of our giving. Tithing was to be a regular, weekly exercise (compare 1 Corinthians 16:2), in which everyone could share and enjoy the adventure, however large or small their income might be, for 'If the willingness is there, the gift is acceptable according to what one has, not according to what he does not have' (2 Corinthians 8:12).

As I warmed to the topic, realising that the implications of stewardship are far broader than just giving money, I launched into a rousing challenge to total commitment – a commitment of our whole life, our time, relationships and abilities.

I felt my first attempt to feed the congregation the full gospel of commitment and stewardship did not go too badly. It had been balanced, I thought; not too harsh, and full of sound theology. I prepared myself for the regular attenders to say, 'Nice sermon, Vicar,' as they shook my hand at the door – and was equally prepared to give the appropriately modest reply: 'Yes, thank you; the devil's told me so already!'

But I was not prepared for the businessman who, while shaking hands, virtually exploded: 'The church is always begging for money, and you're just like all of them! If I want to hear about money, I'll go to my bank manager! You won't be seeing me again. Good day!'

Had I gone over the top? Had I been right before not to have preached about money? On reflection, my answer was 'no' to each question.

'In six years we've had six pastors who were really on fire. We'd like someone lukewarm for a while.'

Not just money

A pig and a hen were passing by a church. Looking up at its noticeboard they saw pinned to it a picture of a person pointing at passersby, asking the question: 'What can *you* do for the poor and needy overseas?'

The hen turned to the pig and cackled enthusiastically: 'I know what we can do, you and I together. We can send them some bacon and eggs!' After a ruminative pause, the pig snorted: 'It's all right for you to make such an outlandish suggestion. Bacon and eggs indeed! For you, a hen, that's only giving a renewable commodity. For me, a pig, it's total commitment!'

Gifts and talents

What do we have that we can give, besides money?

When Jesus told the parable of the talents (Matthew 25:14–30), he reminded his listeners that the man's servants were given different talents to match their abilities. This fits in with Peter's teaching: 'Each one should use whatever gift he has received to serve others, faithfully administering God's grace in its various forms' (1 Peter 4:10).

Time

There is also the question of time, a commodity of which we all have the same allocation. I'm always amazed, though, at how much more other people seem to be able to do with the twenty-four hours they have each day, compared with what I am able to in mine!

'Redeeming the time' (Ephesians 5:16, *KJV*), or 'making the most of every opportunity' (as the *NIV* puts it) seems to be near the top of the list of desirable Christian virtues, judging by the sermons that are preached about it and the jam-packed programmes most churches have! What does it really mean?

● *The Sabbath.* Firstly, for many people, 'giving time to God' means 'doing religious things on Sunday.' The 'specialness' of Sunday is still a significant feature of our national culture, and several Christian organisations are campaigning to keep it so. They see the importance of providing the opportunity for people to give this day to the worship of God. I wonder, though, whether the evangelical wing of the church has not hijacked the sabbath from God's people. In its zeal to 'redeem the time' – especially all that free time on Sundays! – the church has largely lost sight of the need for rest, relaxation, recreation and enjoyment of life.

In New Zealand, we formed a Sunday Club for children

of 'full time' workers like us, for whom Sunday school served up fare that was all too familiar. Each couple took responsibility for a month of Sundays, making up a varied programme of stimulating learning experiences that were good fun. The principle can be translated for an adult group too: learning to celebrate God's creation, enjoy each other's company and discovering the unfamiliar secrets of relaxing, having space and appreciating silence.

I also believe the sabbath principle can be extended into the week from Monday to Saturday: 'taking five' during a busy day; planning space and not feeling guilty about it; enjoying a train journey without feeling the need to read or work (or at least pretend to!); not taking work home from the office, only to bring it back next morning untouched.

● *Assessing priorities.* Secondly, 'redeeming the time' means spending significant amounts of time on those things which are significant for the kingdom of God. The way we use our time inevitably reflects our priorities. We may *think* we live according to certain biblical priorities; if we sit down and chart how we actually spend our time, we will discover whether we really *do* live according to those priorities. For example, few of us would deny that prayer and Bible reading should be very high priorities for the Christian who wants to make an impact on the world. But if we looked honestly at how much time we actually spent in these things, we would be telling a different story. Perhaps many of us should be reversing our television viewing habits with our Bible-reading ones: in other words, reading the Bible for the time we usually give to watching TV, and vice-versa!

Making the most of small slots of time can be an important means of redeeming the time. The cumulative effect of doing small tasks in short time slots, even if it is 'just' planning what needs to be done, can lighten the load of tasks undone. Even crowded train carriages can provide space for thinking time, or when driving home on the motorway late on a Sunday night. I find my mind becomes most productive when, at times like this, it is in neutral!

Establishing priorities

As the church nationwide thinks about stewardship, with so much always waiting to be done and so many opportunities confronting it, the basic problem is that there are so few resources to meet all the needs. Or so we think. Is it really the case? I believe it is, rather, a question of priorities; of what *really* matters to the church, both corporately and individually.

Most countries or cities seem to have a 'Bible-belt'. These are formed of large, healthy, growing, middle-class, wealthy, Bible teaching congregations. They may even be involved in church planting. In recent times in England, I have come across such churches having 'gift days' for church building extensions, when quite phenomenal amounts have been pledged, ranging from £250,000 to £600,000. The same, I know, happens in Australia, America and Canada.

Now growing congregations need the physical plant to cope with the increases in members. But what about the church thirty minutes' drive away? It may be a struggling, deprived, inner city congregation. A handful of committed Christians and a small proportion of the building appeal could make a radical difference to their witness. The same, of course, goes for struggling rural ones. Where should the large churches direct their resources?

Similar problems are also faced by the so-called parachurch organisations. With burgeoning opportunities, almost demanding a strategy of going for growth, an extra staff member can cost £15,000 or more. Is that how the gift income should be spent?

The issue was brought home to some of us recently when we put on a dinner for a number of staff from the two-thirds world, to meet some of our supporting constituency. The latter paid about £4 for the privilege. To our consternation, we learnt that the cost of that meal, when translated into Ugandan shillings, would pay the total salary of a schools' worker in that country for a month! Should we invest that £15,000 in work in Uganda instead?

So, whether we are extending church buildings or recruiting new staff, the problem of prioritising remains the same.

We need to weigh up the best ways in which those talents – whether of time, money or skills and gifts – can be used most effectively for the kingdom. We may need to think especially carefully about two assumptions. Firstly, perhaps 'big' is not always 'best'. And, secondly, sometimes charity, which popular myth would have us believe 'begins at home', may be better disbursed elsewhere!

Prioritising is not simply to do with how we spend our money. A South American Indian was overheard to describe Europeans as 'those white people who worship the God on their wrist'. He'd seen so many look at their watch, and then rush off their next engagement that he had assumed the timepiece held them under its god-like control. He might have extended his description these days to Filofaxes and Psion Electronic Time Managers. The fact is that Christians are as bad, if not worse, than most in allowing themselves to be dominated by *doing*, rather than making time to *be*.

God is the one who gives us all we have and makes us who we are, each of us wonderfully made in his very own image. To be stewards of all that is an awesome responsibility. How do we work out that responsibility in the local church? Certainly, if we want to close it in a decade, we can start by neglecting the basic biblical principles of stewardship. So how can we best apply those principles and motivate our congregations to give genuinely, from the heart?

THE WAY FORWARD

How do we change the levels of commitment in our congregations? There are three aspects to consider.

Broaden the scope of stewardship

Many church members who are reluctant to give to church programmes and charities are often very concerned about the state of the world. We should not equate a lack of enthusiasm for church projects with a general lack of concern or sense of responsibility for others. Far from it! People today are much more aware than ever before of their stewardship responsibilities to the world as a whole. In bringing people to a more fully Christian view of stewardship it is therefore more productive to start with the concerns they already have, than to try to get them to commit themselves to what they see as *your* concerns. So:

Help them meet existing felt responsibilities

Encourage the church as a whole to get involved practically in the concerns of members of its congregation. Perhaps this will involve providing a bottle-bank, encouraging the re-using of tools, clothes and furniture by others when the original owners have no further use for them (a 'swop-shop' or 'good as new' stall), or by helping with a local 'litter-free' campaign. Creative thinking can produce exciting opportunities for involvement with the community, so demonstrating our commitment to a thoughtful stewardship of the earth's resources, and to the values of a non-materialistic lifestyle.

Help overcome a sense of inertia

This takes the first step a bit further. Besides those who are already working for the good of the community, there are many who do nothing, giving the excuse, 'Nothing I do will make any difference.' We must encourage such people to take a share of responsibility for their world and community, 'thinking globally and acting locally'. They could choose to buy 'green' products, walk not drive, avoid impulse buying and seek to minimise waste. Christians do not need to be dictated to by slick advertisements and should not allow their peers to pressurise them into acquiring goods and services which simply pander to pride and status. Individual believers can be encouraged to adopt this lifestyle because it is right – and to persevere in the knowledge that, by being different themselves, they *can* make a difference to society as a whole.

Help overcome misunderstanding of Christian stewardship

Some Christians are put off being committed to a wise use of resources because so much of the green movement seems to be influenced by 'New Age' teaching. Care does need to be taken not to absorb unthinkingly all the ideas that come out of the environmental lobby – some of them are based on principles which are antithetical to biblical Christianity. However, we must not throw out the baby with the organically recycled bin liners! We can lead people on to see that the Bible encourages a proper respect for creation and gives mankind the role of faithful steward within it. If we want to be biblical people we must be wise users of the resources God has given; and if we are using wisely the resources God has given then we are being biblical!

How do we move people on from a general awareness of their stewardship responsibilities to a more specific commitment to the work of the church? Two further elements are involved. The first is an increased commitment to the church family itself; the second is an increased commitment to the work of the church family.

Encourage commitment to the church family

Avoid false measurements of commitment
Attendance at meetings ought not to be the major criterion for assessing commitment. Long working days, commuting and unsociable hours can all add to the pressures on modern family life. Most churches could happily keep the average family with 2.4 children out at meetings five nights a week. It is better, instead, to have a high level of commitment to a selected, small number of meetings.

Strengthen membership requirements
The pressure is to do the opposite of this – 'Let's make it easier, not have such high standards, expect less.' Experience, however, shows that when we spell out the serious nature of commitment to the local church, indicate the level of dedication we are looking for and ask for a thoughtful, sacrificial response, people respond positively. We all prefer to belong to something worth joining; an organisation which takes itself, and us, seriously.

Involve people more quickly
Some churches still have a rule that you can't be a leader until you've been part of the congregation for five years. As most city suburbs have a population that moves on average

every three years, it's hardly surprising that there is a shortage of leaders! We need to be able to discern gifts and abilities in newcomers quickly, and then give them scope to operate (see Chapter 9). We must move from a position of giving people responsible jobs when we feel they have earned it (by length of stay, etc) to a position where we can allocate jobs on the basis of character and gifting. We will sometimes make mistakes here, but sensitive follow-up of someone in a new role will minimise the impact of any mistakes they may be making. People are much more likely to be committed to a church where they feel they have a valuable contribution to make.

Help commitment to be 'caught' as well as taught!
As leaders we must not only teach commitment, we must *be* committed ourselves. Without this personal example, members of the congregation are likely to feel fairly unmotivated by even the most brilliant sermons on commitment!

As leaders, our own commitment must be reflected in a willingness to consider a long-term stay in the community. The average tenure of clergy in Britain appears to be less than three years! If this is the case, it's no wonder church members find it difficult to treat what their leaders say seriously. After all, they're probably going to get a new leader soon, with different ideas, plans and projects to which he will want their 'commitment'. A significant number of leaders will have to be ready to put down their roots in a particular community for an extended period of time; if we are to see genuine commitment among ordinary church members.

From his experience in the Anglican ministry, David adds that in his last parish he had hoped to carry out a generational ministry, marrying as adults the babies he had baptised. But it was not to be; a move came after eight years. He is sure it was right to move then, but commitment was total while he was there. It is true that commitment cannot be measured for the leader in terms of years any more than it can be for the more mobile church members. However, God *does* seem to call his people for an extended period of time to some particular situations – such as the inner city – where the tasks of building bridges and gaining trust require a long-term stay.

Commitment to the work of the church family

God calls his church to be adventurous in its work with him in the world. How can we help church members be enthused by this and give sacrificially to see God's work go forward?

- *Be inspirational!* Church leaders need to create the vision of what can be done, the good that can be achieved, the people that can be brought into the kingdom. And the congregation needs to be convinced! People won't give if they are not convinced that the leaders have hit on real needs, or doubt their competence to see a project through.
- *Give specific information.* People give better to people and 'causes' rather than to keep an institution going. Highlight specific needs on the mission field, a definite and clearly defined crisis in the church, or target a family for special help. Explain 'why' a project needs to be done. Help folk to see what their money will achieve.
- *Involve the congregation.* The greater the congregational 'ownership' of a project, the more generous and committed their giving is likely to be. The congregation should be involved in the decision-making process of what aspect of wider ministry the church should be involved in. Ask them, too, how they would like to be informed about the church's own financial needs. Involve them in identifying appropriate fund raising methods and the setting of financial goals.
- *Be open about money!* Don't be afraid to talk to people *personally* about their giving – especially when they are looking at ways of becoming more involved in the church. Be sensitive, not manipulative, but direct. Money should not be a 'no-go' area in pastoral conversations.
- *Provide information on how to give.* Display offering envelopes, a standing order agreement and a covenant form. Identify an individual who is available to talk through people's personal circumstances and will help them fill the forms in!
- *Teach about stewardship.* This must come with gentleness and integrity. High-pressure sales techniques may produce a one-off response but not long-term systematic giving. Study the subject of stewardship – of money, gifts and time – in house groups. Recommend appropriate books and tapes

and encourage a regular (at least annual) reassessment of giving in each of these areas.

- *Be aware of real financial problems.* A growing barrier to Christians increasing the level of their giving is the problem of debt. It is possible that around ten percent of our congregation could be in serious financial straits. This problem will be with us at least for the first half of this decade. We must offer practical support and help with planning budgets. Crucially, we must urge people to ask for help as the problems begin, not wait until crisis point! This is the other side of the 'stewardship' coin: the church fellowship and its leaders are responsible for the welfare of its members just as much as they are responsible for how they use their money.

If the church is to make a significant impact this decade it will have to call for a deeper level of commitment from its members, including a rededication of all our resources to God for use in his work.

> 'Jesus for Thee a body takes,
> Thy guilt assumes, Thy fetters break,
> Discharging all Thy dreadful debt;
> And canst Thou e'er such love forget?'
> *Krishna Pal*

13

Evangelism: Do or Die!

THE ISSUES

The motorway system in the United Kingdom was one of the facts of life to which we had to adapt when we moved here from Australia. I listened to a radio programme not long ago where people who worked in the service areas on the motorways were being interviewed. They were saying it was as if they were in an oasis. Drivers and passengers arrive dazed, having been sitting in a car, speeding along sometimes for hundreds of miles, then they come into what is euphemistically called a 'comfort stop'. Their behaviour can be bizarre and irrational, as they rapidly withdraw from the enclosed cell of their speeding box!

The purpose of the church

The 'comfort stop' or 'service station' is an appropriate description for what the church often sees itself to be, although that is only part of the picture. As we have already noted, the church is meant to 'comfort the disturbed and to disturb the comfortable', and a balanced gospel diet will do both. The hell-fire and brimstone caricature which knows only how to disturb the comfortable is, thankfully, not as common as once it was, but perhaps the pendulum has swung too far in the other direction. Prosperity theology and its varied heresies go over the top in comforting the already too comfortable adherents to the cause.

Commitment to evangelism

J B Phillips commented that the early Christians 'were led by the Spirit to the main task of bringing people to Christ and were not permitted to enjoy fascinating sidetracks.' Yet today even the most outgoing local church finds it difficult to maintain a focus on evangelism. Time, money and resources are so easily drawn into sustaining the programme of activities for those already committed, maintaining the building they meet in and caring for their pastoral needs. If we were to examine most church budgets this would become fairly clear. No doubt first-century accounts would tell a different story!

'Evangelism' has become a project to *do* from time to time, rather than a life to be lived all the time. It is a project that often exhausts the church, amuses the devil and annoys the community! No wonder we shy away from it and need to be called back to it. Yet it is fairly obvious that if the church does not evangelise it will eventually, and surely, die.

Jesus' great commission was the first 'call to evangelism': 'Therefore go and make disciples of all nations, baptising them in the name of the Father and of the Son and of the Holy Spirit, and teaching them to obey everything I have commanded you' (Matthew 28:19). Simply stated, evangelism is sharing good news. The caricature of an evangelist is that of an arrogant, abrasive salesman pushing a package down the metaphorical throat of an unwilling customer. The reality is, as someone has described it: 'I'm simply one starving beggar telling another beggar where to find bread.'

The vast majority of us in the local church need to take a long, hard look at ourselves and have the courage to ask where evangelism is in our list of priorities. This can fairly quickly be gauged by the answers to specific questions, such as:

● How much money do we allocate for evangelism?
● Which of our meetings/organisations is evangelistic in focus?
● For how many people in the church family is evangelism their main 'job responsibility'?

The answers are likely to reveal that we think evangelism is

179

important only in theory. The practice reveals where our actual priorities are.

Key principles

Many things hold churches back from being a witnessing community – internal conflict, lack of vision, pursuing other priorities, fear. If we are to motivate our congregations to move out in evangelism, there are three key principles we need to be teaching. Lots of otherwise 'successful' churches do not get anywhere much in evangelism, either because the church family is confused about them or has simply not 'heard' them.

1 Knowing Jesus

Evangelism is all about introducing people to Jesus. But we can't introduce people to someone we don't know ourselves. So the first requirement for effective evangelism is clearly that those who call themselves Christians should *know* Jesus and have a living relationship with him. When the church spends its energies on making sure its members know all *about* Jesus, rather than knowing *him*, its efforts to evangelise will be severely hindered. As an elderly missionary in Mauritius used to say to us: 'There are many people who miss out on eternity by eighteen inches. They have Jesus here (pointing to the brain), but not here (pointing to the heart).' The church often communicates a cerebral rather than an experiential understanding of Jesus.

The church can also give the impression that evangelism is 'being done' if people are being drawn into the life of the church. That is not necessarily so. People may be sucked into the church, as though it were a big vacuum cleaner, and *still* not know – or be introduced to – Jesus. People looking for friendship and 'an outside interest' can be sucked into our round of religious activities, rather than be drawn to Jesus himself. This 'vacuum cleaner' mentality expects people to come to us on our terms, so avoiding putting ourselves out by doing what Christ commanded: 'Go . . . make disciples.'

The vacuum cleaner mentality would be fine if, once people were in the fellowship, they stayed in. But the statistics are cruel. People who have been sucked in on this basis, have tried what the church has to offer and then turned away from it, are much harder to reach than before.

Whatever the reasons may be (and not all blame or fault can be laid at the church's door) we have to admit that some of the church's evangelistic endeavours have been ludicrously irrelevant.

My years with the Bible Society showed me that the Bible is one of our most potent resources, a powerful means of evangelism. I know so many stories of people whose lives have been changed simply through reading the Bible, that I would always encourage others to let it loose in evangelism. It speaks supremely of Jesus, and will do so in a way that introduces the reader to him, specifically and personally. All the systems and programmes in the world, all the formulae and strategies for evangelism we may ever devise, can never replace the transforming power of a living relationship with Christ. If our churches are to *survive* the decade, let alone grow through evangelism, that's where we need to focus our energies first. Then there will be the motivation and the resources to win our generation for Christ.

2 The reality of judgment

We need a re-emphasis on judgment. Jesus was under no illusion as to its reality and neither ought we to be. Of course we will want to avoid some of the crude 'hell-fire' techniques employed by a number of preachers in the past. And of course we will want to express this truth with sadness and gentleness. But having said this, we must *express* this truth. Most of the great waves of evangelistic fervour in church history were significantly motivated by a clear understanding of the fate of those who rejected Christ. When God's judgment of sin is not a feature of our preaching and teaching we effectively destroy a major source of motivation toward evangelism. When our churches are gripped with the knowledge of the destiny of those around them, a new urgency affects their ministry.

I believe that we dare not minimise this. God's judgment on sin is not a 'fringe' doctrine in the Bible (it is mentioned specifically at least fifty times). Nor must we allow our late

twentieth-century distaste for the subject to obscure the truth.
C S Lewis helpfully identifies the heart of the issue:

> 'In the long run, the answer to all those who object to the doctrine of hell, is itself a question: "what are you asking God to do?" To wipe out their past sins and, at all costs, to give them a fresh start, smoothing every difficulty and offering every miraculous help? But he has done so on Calvary. To forgive them? They will not be forgiven. To leave them alone? Alas, that is what he does.'
>
> (C S Lewis, *Mere Christianity*, London: Collins, 1970.)

We will always want to be pastorally sensitive when we speak of hell, always cautious not to say *more* than the Bible says and never gloating over the destiny of those who reject God. Nevertheless, we are unlikely to see hundreds of ordinary, local churches fired with evangelistic passion without a return to an acceptance of this doctrine.

3 Personal responsibility

Thirdly, we need a new emphasis on the personal responsibility of individual believers to evangelise. For thousands of Christians, the teaching of recent years on spiritual gifts and ministries, though excellent in itself, has been used to avoid personal responsibility to share the good news: 'Evangelism is a spiritual gift and the "evangelist" is a ministry-calling. I don't have either the gift or the ministry, so I have no responsibility for evangelism. My gifts lie elsewhere.' This is a dangerous half-truth which has led many Christians to abdicate their responsibility for winning their bit of the world to Christ, passing on the job to others whose role they perceive it to be. While continuing to teach on spiritual gifts, we must reassert that it is both the privilege and the responsibility of *every* believer to bear witness to their faith.

THE WAY FORWARD

Leighton Ford has defined evangelism as comprising presence, proclamation and persuasion. Though it is probably 'persuasion' that ultimately 'clinches the deal' and brings a person to decision and commitment, all three elements are usually needed in the process. In the final analysis, of course, conversions are brought about by the Holy Spirit: we could call this 'power' evangelism.

The fear many of us have with any designated decade, even for such a vital one as evangelism, is that programmes will predominate, and the *doing* of the exercise will become more important than the *being* of the people of God. God's means of drawing people to himself has always been, and always will be, people. No amount of literature, recourse to sophisticated forms of communication, activity, or the hiring of gifted preachers, can ever substitute for personal relationships. 'Presence', 'proclamation', 'persuasion' and even 'power' evangelism only work effectively as partners of 'personal' evangelism.

Each of these emphases highlights a different dimension of our *personal* evangelistic task:

• Presence evangelism is the *context* for personal evangelism.
• Proclamation evangelism is the *content* of personal evangelism.
• Persuasion evangelism is the *craft* of personal evangelism.
• Power evangelism is the *cutting edge* of personal evangelism.

This means that our task as local churches is to help provide these emphases corporately in order that effective evangelism can be carried out personally.

Presence evangelism

Presence evangelism is to do with being, with living out our faith in a way that will attract others to Jesus. It is being honest, available, being God's person. As Dick Innes put it, 'by virtue of the fact that I am a Christian, I am automatically a witness for Jesus Christ.' (Dick Innes, *I Hate Witnessing*. Ventura: Regal Books, 1983)

Some have felt that presence evangelism is a cop-out for 'the real thing', by which they normally mean a clearly defined formula of stages which must be explained to the potential convert. These will generally lead them from an awareness of sin, through confusion and repentance, to making a decision to follow Christ as Lord and Saviour. The hard truth is that living a life that is a consistent witness for Christ – in the home, at school, work and in the world day in, day out – is far more demanding than trotting out well-worn formulae or clichés at inappropriate times. Presence evangelism demands consistency, honesty and maturity. People know intuitively that 'being' is more important than doing or saying. When they see an attractive, Christian life lived consistently, the effect can be very powerful.

I guess many of us harbour feelings of guilt about not being more effective evangelistic witnesses. Dick Innes' excellent book, *I Hate Witnessing* (see above), reflects what I suspect most of us feel! But Dick is a real encourager. He points out that, even among the twelve disciples hand-picked by Jesus, probably only one of them had the gift of an evangelist. It was Andrew. He was the one who introduced Peter to Jesus. He found the boy with the loaves and fish and brought him to Jesus. And he was the one who introduced the Greek enquirers to Jesus.

But what he did is something we can all do. He didn't use a special formula. No methodology. No programme. He simply introduced them to Jesus. That same Jesus said, 'I, when I am lifted up from the earth, will draw all men to myself' (John 12:32). It is true that Jesus said this in order to show the kind of death he was going to die, but it is also true that when Jesus is 'lifted up', and shown in clarity for who he is, he does draw people to himself.

Presence evangelism: how to go about it

Individually

Relationships don't just happen; they need time and opportunity. Most Christians are so busy in the church that they don't have time to have any 'presence' in the community. As churches we must release people *from* meetings and release them *into* the community. We need to streamline our administration, avoid duplication of meetings and may need to change expectations in the church about attendance at activities and events.

Evangelism is tricky if you don't know many non-Christians! Large parts of the church family are in this position. Collectively, we will have to simplify our church structures, and individually we will have to alter our lifestyles, if we are to get to know more non-Christians. If we are honest, most of us are operating on the principle of 'absence' evangelism as far as our relationships with non-Christians are concerned!

As a church
The vast majority of local churches find themselves in communities which are not sympathetic to their mission, although there is often a residual sympathy for the church and a sentimental allegiance to some religious concepts. We are surrounded by nice people (in the main) who have little antagonism towards the church but who have largely dismissed it as of little contemporary relevance. It's a 'minority interest', 'OK if you like that sort of thing', but most are quite happy to have it in the community in case they ever need it. They might want to be married there or expect to be buried there, but generally don't anticipate much contact with it between those events.

The first task for the local church, therefore, it to raise the 'God-consciousness' of its surrounding community. Somehow the church has to be drawn to the attention of the people around it – moved from the edge to the centre of their consciousness. Here are some ways to do this:

● *Give the church building a 'face-lift'*. Repair the fence, repaint the exterior, put up a notice board – all these things indicate signs of life!
● *Advertise your services in the local paper*. Give frequent press releases about what the church is doing.
● *Distribute a magazine* to all the homes in your area. Have a special feature for the elderly and another for children. Share church and community news. Include 'low-key' testimonies.
● *Contribute to a community project*. Enlist volunteers to help in a local hospice, school for the blind, or whatever the local needs might be. Sponsor a park bench or the flowers in

the council-maintained roundabout. Start a Neighbourhood Watch scheme.

● *Meet a community need.* Run a luncheon club for the elderly, start a 'parents and toddlers' group, organise a day out for the 'shut-ins' or open an Advice Centre.

● *Hold a community event.* Have a community carol concert, either in the open air or in a hired public building, like the sports centre. Arrange a craft fair or 'fun-festival' during the school holidays.

None of these things are directly 'evangelistic' but they alert the community to the existence and relevance of God's people. We become a group that *does* things of obvious value. Our genuine care for the community gives us a platform from which the gospel can be presented. It is much more readily received when the church proclaiming it is already a credible concern.

Proclamation evangelism

Far too many of us think we have engaged in evangelism when we have really only been involved in pre-evangelism. However, sooner or later, the good news must be shared in an understandable way; this involves telling someone about Jesus, about some aspect of what he has done for me and will do for all who trust him:

> 'How, then, can they call on the one they have not believed in? And how can they believe in the one of whom they have not heard? And how can they hear without someone preaching to them?' *Romans 10:14–15*

Just as the principle applies to preaching in general, so it applies to evangelism in particular: 'You also must testify, for you have been with me from the beginning' (John 15:27), Jesus exhorted the disciples. The angel told the imprisoned, persecuted apostles to 'Go . . . and tell the people the full message of this new life' (Acts 5:20). Peter, writing to God's people scattered throughout the known world, laid it on the line: 'in your hearts, set apart Christ as Lord. Always be prepared to give an answer to everyone who asks you to give the reason for the hope that you have. But do this with gentleness and respect . . .' (1 Peter 3:15).

Credibility, authenticity and sensitivity seem to be the marks of effective evangelism. Michael Green, in his classic *Evangelism in the Early Church* (Crowborough: Highland Books, 1984), describes the main method of that early church as being 'gossiping the gospel', sharing the good news in the natural environment of their daily lives. And here we see how close is the link between 'presence' and 'proclamation'. Innes points out that Jesus didn't say to his disciples, 'After the Holy Spirit is given to you, you will go out and *do* witnessing.' Rather he said, 'After you receive the Holy Spirit, you will *be* witnesses to me' (Acts 1:8; see Innes, *I Hate Witnessing*, p 32). Who they were, and how they lived, was vital to the effectiveness of what they said.

And what I do will certainly affect how others respond to what I want to share with them: in this case, the good news. But I do what I do because I am what I am, which is why Jesus warned us clearly, 'by their fruit you will recognise them' (Matthew 7:20). What people see of me is a reflection of who I really am, so that to do effective evangelism, we need to be effective evangelists. Proclamation *alone* is of little use – although God can use it! – if our inner life is not integrated with our outer life. That's what integrity is all about. How many of us would dare to say, like Paul, 'imitate me' (1 Corinthians 4:16)?

Proclamation evangelism: how to go about it

What to say

Once we have established a relationship, what do we actually say? Many Christians need training in this area. To supplement their own experiences of Christ we must help people articulate their faith, guide them to key aspects of the gospel story and point out some relevant passages and verses.

Four basic points are worth remembering:

- Everyone has fallen short of God's standard (Romans 3:23).
- Only Jesus can help us reach God's standard (John 14:6).
- We must say sorry to God and turn our back on wrong (2 Peter 3:9).

• Jesus wants to forgive us, put us right with God and give us a fresh start (2 Corinthians 5:17).

There is no shortage of other systems and programmes, ranging from Evangelism Explosion (which provides helpful conversation starters and probing questions), through the Four Spiritual Laws (a set formula, like that above, for presenting the basics of the gospel), to training programmes like *Person to Person* (a video training programme, produced by Scripture Union, Campus Crusade and the Bible Society). Each of these, and many others beside, provide good material to help get us going. But none will work without the involvement of people – people like you and me, and those with whom we want to share the good news. Evangelism is *always* people, not programmes.

David writes: The first time I saw Evangelism Explosion put into practice, it nearly blew my mind! It was at a church weekend in New Zealand at which I had been invited to lead the Bible studies. The topic was evangelism, and they were going to 'do it' between the teaching sessions. The minister coordinating the weekend was shy and stuttering, comparatively inarticulate, but godly and sold on the concept of evangelism. He was to take a small group – which included me – out into the community to show us how he did it. It was Sunday morning. We approached a house where a man was working on his car engine in the garage at the back. What he thought of the minister and three of us arriving unannounced I can only guess! But within minutes, the conversation had deftly turned to matters of more eternal concern than a car engine, and we were all invited in for a cup of coffee. Within half an hour, he had made what seemed an absolutely genuine, unpressured commitment to Christ, with the fundamental questions of the faith having been clearly dealt with in a conversational manner.

Learning from others

A church-run mission can be very useful because it gives Christians the chance to hear the gospel presented by an 'expert', and gives non-Christian friends a chance to hear the good news from a different angle. It can also provide the opportunity for discussion between the Christian and his or her friend.

People who don't profess any Christian faith will often be happy to read a book or watch a video which explains the faith, if given to them by someone they are getting to know and trust. Again, if sensitively followed up with questions like, 'What did you make of that?' 'Was there anything you didn't quite follow?' a helpful discussion can get going.

There are many other church-based or church-run events which 'novice' evangelists can participate in and so learn from:

- evangelistic discussion groups;
- coffee evenings with a special speaker;
- lunches, with a well-known person coming to talk about what it means to them to be a Christian;
- a seminar with a Christian 'slant' – perhaps on marriage or debt;
- a Christian play or drama evening;
- a concert given by a Christian musician who will also talk a bit about his or her Christian commitment;
- an open evening at a local bookshop with a Christian author as the guest and speaker.

Persuasion evangelism

Persuasion evangelism is not another term for proselytism – the attempt to convert others to our particular party tag or denomination! But it does denote determination and hard work put towards achieving a specific goal. John Stott puts it like this:

'To evangelise is to proclaim God's good news about Jesus Christ to the end that people will believe in him, find life in him, and ultimately be conformed to his image, not ours.' (John Stott, *I Believe in Preaching*. London: Hodder, 1982.)

Most of us would accept such a statement – in theory. It could become the guiding definition for this decade. But we seem to be afraid of the persuasive, determined aspect. We have lost our nerve. We are afraid to evangelise for fear of being seen as Victorian fanatics. So we have ended up with the opposite scenario. The media delight in lampooning the church and its leaders as they bend over backwards to make the gospel *acceptable* to this generation. We water it down and demand only minimal commitment, if any, trying our best to 'make it relevant'.

Some of the gobbledegook that results would be hilarious if it weren't so serious. Interestingly, the early church didn't try to *make* the gospel relevant to secular society. They grasped the fact that the gospel *is* dynamically relevant, to each succeeding generation, in all situations. Humanity's basic needs are always the same, and the solutions held out to us in the gospel are the only ones that answer those needs.

Stephen didn't lose his nerve when he was arrested and ultimately martyred. He continued to speak persuasively: 'They could not stand up against his wisdom or the Spirit by whom he spoke' (Acts 6:10). Philip unashamedly seized his opportunity to explain the scriptures to the Ethiopian eunuch he met on the Gaza strip in the desert (Acts 8:30–35). In Corinth, Paul's approach to evangelism was typical: 'Every Sabbath he reasoned in the synagogue, trying to persuade Jews and Greeks' (Acts 18:4).

Persuasion evangelism, then, comes from being sold on the message ourselves, from having a deep devotion to the person of Christ, a concern for the need of the hearers, and a loving burden to share the good news. It is presenting the gospel in such a way as to provoke a verdict!

Persuasion evangelism: how to go about it

Persuading people to become Christians is ultimately the responsibility of the Holy Spirit. From the human point of view, however, there are two major things involved in being a persuasive communicator:
• *A winsome personality and attitude.* We must be humble, honest about our own failings and not patronising. Being genuine has an enormously convincing effect; but we must be 'genuinely genuine' or those we talk with will spot it a mile off!

● *The art of apologetics.* Apologetics is about understanding why our faith is reasonable and discovering the evidence which supports it. And there is a great deal! (See resources list at back of book.) Far too many popular objections to Christianity are allowed to go unchallenged. Presuppositions must be questioned, 'silly' arguments demolished and logical grounds for the rationality of the Christian faith established. All this must be done gently, but firmly. Most Christians aren't aware how sensible their faith is!

For example, despite its popularity, 'you can believe what you like as long as you're sincere' is nonsense. Try sincerely believing that you can live without breathing! Yes, people can be sincerely wrong. Similarly, 'science has disproved Christianity,' 'Jesus never existed,' 'The Bible is full of contradictions,' etc, can all be disproved by careful attention to the facts.

'Pastor, I'd like you to meet my husband, Carl, who decided to come to church this Sunday.'

Providing the cutting edge

No personal evangelism will succeed without the power of God. Christians must be dependent on God, rather than any training, technique or personality strength. Only his power can bring people from darkness to light. Our evangelism must be bathed in prayer, to this end.

We must help one another to develop an expectancy that God's power will break loose as we witness: bringing deep conviction, the expulsion of evil forces and physical or emotional healing. Jesus is alive and active today!

The focus of the local church in the Decade of Evangelism is to prepare all the people of God for the task of spreading the good news; having been prepared, we should encourage and enable them to *do* it!

> 'Send forth the gospel! Let it run
> Southward and northward, east and west:
> Tell all the earth Christ died and lives,Who
> giveth pardon, life, and rest.'
> *Henry Fox*

14

Mission

THE ISSUES

In his striking parable of the sheep and the goats Jesus shows unequivocably the prime importance he places on social concerns, especially for the so-called 'underside' of society:

'I tell you the truth, whatever you did for one of the least of these brothers of mine, you did for me . . .

I was hungry and you gave me nothing to eat, I was thirsty and you gave me nothing to drink, I was a stranger and you did not invite me in, I needed clothes and you did not clothe me, I was sick and in prison, and you did not look after me . . .

I tell you the truth, whatever you did not do for one of the least of these, you did not do for me.'

Matthew 25:40, 42–43, 45

Evangelism or social action?

I have never fully understood the battles that have been fought, even within the evangelical traditions of the church, between those who believe the church's task is evangelism and those who believe it is social action. It has always seemed obvious to me that 'mission' involves both. It is one of those 'both/and' situations, rather than an 'either/or'.

Although Martin Luther may well have called the letter of James 'an epistle of straw', he could not have argued with its central thesis, that faith without works is not the genuine article. Jesus, in the parable quoted above, placed such store by the good works that showed evidence of underlying faith, that he indicated our eternal destiny depended on what we do or don't do: 'Then they will go away to eternal punishment, but the righteous to eternal life' (Matthew 25:46).

If the church is to survive the decade with any credibility, it will need to reaffirm that our witness to the world has to be both by word *and* by deed. We cannot separate the two. Our lives have to reflect the truths we proclaim. This will never deny that the source of our salvation is God's grace, that the ground of our salvation is Jesus Christ, that the means of our salvation is faith; but the evidence of our salvation will be our works. What's more, people's readiness to *hear* the good news often depends on how clearly they can *see* it. As the African proverb so aptly puts it: 'An empty belly has no ears.'

'The work of the church is outside the establishment. Outside the church. In the world. And it takes every member to do it! Nowhere in the Bible is the world exhorted to "come to church". But the church's mandate is clear: she must go to the world.' (Richard Halverson.) There is little doubt that this principle is one of the most vital for the church to grasp as we head for the end of the century. We must be healed from the dreaded disease of in-growing eye-balls and begin to see the scope of the mission field. And it is immense. For starters, there is still an urgent need for missionary activity in every country on all five continents! And even if we assume a fair degree of success in the middle classes (which we can't!) and stop ministering to the affluent suburbs (which we shouldn't!) why don't we reach out to the other extremes of the very rich and very poor? (Because we daren't!)

There are very small numbers of Christians among the wealthy in our world. Jesus himself indicated what a hindrance money could be to entry into his kingdom. Nevertheless, this is almost an 'unreached people group'; especially in Europe. But of course, the wealthy are only a very small percentage of the total population. There are millions who are desperately poor around the world – hundreds of thousands in our own country. And there are thousands more who are 'poor' in the biblical sense: alienated, with no access to power, defeated and discouraged. They could be single parents, homeless teenagers, victims of abuse, the institutionalised elderly, AIDS sufferers, those in ethnic minority groups, handicapped and house-bound people, addicts, those in prison, the mentally disturbed, frightened, confused – and those who are simply sad and alone.

For the vast majority of these people the church is an irrelevance; which is an uncomfortable reminder of how far we have come since Jesus was criticised for his associations with the 'underside' of society (Matthew 11:19), commanded action among the outcasts and those who are hurting (Matthew 25:34f), and whose ministry evoked the shocked response, 'This man welcomes sinners and eats with them!' (Luke 15:2.) The local churches of our country must get back to the ministry of their Founder.

The need for clear thinking
Historically, evangelicals have changed society, influencing people everywhere in the battle against slavery and in the quest for social justice. Where would we be without the Wilberforces, the Shaftesburys, the Booths and the Wesleys? And yet conflicts and dichotomies remain.

In the excellent book, *In Word and Deed: Evangelism and Social Responsibility* (ed Bruce Nicholls, Exeter: Paternoster, 1985), Tokunboh Adeyemo helpfully lists nine conflicting options for evangelicals (p 48ff):

- that social action is a *distraction* from evangelism
- that social action is a *betrayal* of evangelism
- that social action is *evangelism*
- that social action is a *means* to evangelism
- that social action is a *manifestation* of evangelism
- that social action is a *result* or consequence of evangelism
- that social action is a *partner* of evangelism
- that social action and evangelism are equally important but genuinely distinct aspects of the total mission of the church
- that social action is *part* of evangelism

Although there are those who would still hold to one or other of the first two options, there does appear to have been a major shift in thinking and practice in recent times. The Lausanne movement may well have been a major factor contributing to that shift, but there is profuse biblical encouragement to see social action as integral to evangelism, and hence to the overall mission of the church.

The parable of the good Samaritan (Luke 10:25–37) leaves us in no doubt. It was the priest and the Levite who failed the test, but the unlikely Samaritan whose care and compassion we are urged to emulate: 'Go and do likewise', Jesus said.

'Bias to the poor'

In the Beatitudes given in the Sermon on the Mount (Matthew 5:1–12), and particularly in the parallel blessings and woes in Luke's Gospel (Luke 6:20–26), there seems to be good evidence for what David Sheppard has controversially called 'bias to the poor' (see David Sheppard, *Bias to the Poor*. London: Hodder & Stoughton, 1983). Note the contrasts that Luke draws:

> 'Blessed are you who are poor . . . woe to you who are rich.'
> 'Blessed are you who hunger now . . . woe to you who are well fed now . . .'

This must have been shocking to the ears of Jesus' listeners, accustomed as they were to the prosperity emphasis of much of what we now call the Old Testament.

Although Jesus was making a particular point to the rich ruler who was asking what he had to do to inherit eternal life, nonetheless his need was to sell what he had and to give the proceeds to the poor, so that he might have treasure in heaven. His material well-being was, in his case, the barrier to his following Jesus (Luke 18:18–30).

Real needs to be met

When he was at a prominent Pharisee's house for a meal, Jesus took the opportunity to tell the guests a parable, making the point directly to his host:

When you give a banquet, invite the poor, the crippled, the lame, the blind, and you will be blessed. Although they cannot repay you, you will be repaid at the resurrection of the righteous.'

Luke 14:13

We found ourselves unwillingly put in such a situation one Christmas. At our church, we determined to put on a special meal on Christmas Day, for all those who would be on their own: the single, widows and widowers, those living lonely lives in apartments and rooms, so they would have an enjoyable day.

To our astonishment, we had scarcely any takers! Nearly all those we imagined would come from the church congregation had made arrangements to be with friends or relatives. So, in true biblical fashion (motivated by the fact that all the catering arrangements had been made), we went out into the highways and byways inviting passersby to come and join us for the feast. There was bemused amazement, but much fun and enjoyment, and we certainly experienced Jesus' assurance that we would be blessed!

How comfortable would the 'underside' of society feel in our churches and congregations? Aren't they the very people whose needs lay closest to Jesus' heart? In what has come to be called 'the Nazareth manifesto,' Jesus used the Scripture reading in the context of the synagogue service to provide his own 'job description':

'The Spirit of the Lord is on me,
   because he has anointed me
   to preach good news to the poor.
He has sent me to proclaim
   freedom for the prisoners
   and recovery of sight for the blind,
to release the oppressed,
   to proclaim the year of the Lord's favour.'

Luke 4:18–19

I was impressed recently to observe a 'Dirty Hands' tour in England, which was encouraging Christians literally to get their hands dirty in God's work of redeeming a lost, broken and oppressed world. As one lives and works in the inner cities of the world, it is difficult to deny what Malcolm Muggeridge once described as the 'advanced stage of decomposition' of western civilisation. With its 'big bangs' and city frauds, its focus on finance and its preoccupation with power, the world seems to be forgetting that Jesus is the prophet of the loser's camp, not the victor's, proclaiming that the first will be last, that the weak are the strong and the fools the wise; and that the poor and lowly, not the rich and proud, possess the kingdom of heaven.

Our Scripture Union head office is based within walking distance of the fabulous City of London, one of the greatest financial centres of the world; yet it also borders the edge of the East End of London. Within a mile radius of our building, there is a microcosm of that world for which Jesus cared so much that he died for it. I can imagine him weeping over it, as he did over Jerusalem.

In the churchyard where we have been allowed to park our cars, there are piles of window glass from the many cars that have been broken into. Just today, as I write, a young policeman was shot dead in one of the housing estates, as he disturbed a car thief. Such estates can be vast, impersonal, concrete deserts of despair, where the people have become simply statistics. They are barely able to survive in environments of such squalor and decay.

Unemployment continues to be an unwelcome scourge in lives that have such potential to offer society. Homeless beggars, some of them young, ask for loose change in the underground. For some, admittedly, it is an easy way to pay for their addiction, but that certainly is not the motivation for all. A mission hospital, also within walking distance, has been quietly but effectively working with AIDS victims. In the same area is the Spitalfields Crypt, where people work to show Christ's care and compassion for homeless alcoholics or 'vagrants', as the statistics label them with such insensitive lack of dignity.

How can we make any difference?

Can the church make inroads of any kind into this 'underside' of our society? Historically, we have made little impact. Statistically and sociologically, we show little evidence of attempting to, at least in western countries. It is sobering to realise that in what we call 'third world' countries – such as in Asia, Africa and Latin America, and in more recent days in Eastern and Central Europe – where the church is growing most rapidly, it is amongst the 'underside' that the greatest inroads are being made.

Just as I wrote that last sentence the telephone rang. It was a young man who had worked with our Street Level project, alongside the churches within a mile's radius of the office. He had just come back from a period in Mexico City, working amongst a community of one thousand urban families. 'Revival is breaking out!' he exclaimed with obvious excitement, as he asked whether he could use our fax machine to get an urgent message through to them!

It may be that the church has to break out of its 'pew-warming' mentality, where people are seen as either 'church-goers' or 'non-churchgoers', and vast energies are expended to convert the latter into the former. One of the churches in which we worked decided to employ a full-time youth worker. He was to work with young people who rarely, if ever, came to church: unemployed, homeless, drug addicts. Part of the deal was that he was not to feel guilty if there were no additions to the congregation – although some of the church members found that difficult to swallow!

It was a long, hard row to hoe, and even now, many years later, some fruit of his work is only beginning to mature. It was over two years before any of the young people he reached would come even into the churchyard, let alone the church! But this 'no strings attached' style of ministry was one of integrity that slowly formed the building blocks of trust on which faith could ultimately be built.

The challenge of a plural society

Still within easy walking distance of the office, in this multifa-ceted corner of London's vast metropolis, live no fewer than 80,000 Bangladeshi immigrants and their families. They reflect the increasingly common global trend towards multi-cultural societies. Marshall McLuhan's 'global village' has become a reality, with people of different cultures and creeds having to co-exist with each other, often uneasily.

The mosques and churches of London's East End sit on streets whose Jewish names reflect the trade of an earlier age. They symbolise that multicultural pluralism with which our churches must come to grips if they are to survive the decade. In an age where tolerance sometimes seems to be the supreme virtue, a robust but sensitive grasp of Christian apologetics is sorely needed. Paul, who was happy to debate and persuade in the Athenian Areopagus, would feel at home in most cities of the world today. Some commentators feel his outreach at the Areopagus failed because only 'a few men' are said to have come to faith there (Acts 17:34). But Paul met them on their own ground, reaching out to them, building bridges, and was unafraid to declare the reality of the resurrection.

The challenges of pluralism and a multifaith society are possibly the greatest ones the church faces this decade. In a generation where tolerance and sincerity are upheld as the cardinal virtues, no matter what you believe, the claim that Jesus alone is the way, the truth and the life (John 14:6) is perceived as arrogant, and destructive of social peace. Yet the task of the church is to continue to proclaim that only through Jesus do we find the way to the Father, and by his name alone can we be saved (Acts 4:12).

Many people are being drawn into aspects of the New Age movement. They are attracted to the transcendent dimension of eastern mysticism and are often reacting against the spiritual emptiness of cerebral religion and the shallowness of materialism. This compounds the challenges of the alternate world faiths that earlier generations knew about only in the abstract. The longer the church puts off dealing with these beliefs, the more rapid the decline of the church's influence will be.

We need to regain our nerve, to renew our confidence in the gospel, and to live Christ in our generation. We need to reject the siege mentality that so often surfaces as majority movements dwindle into a minority. Instead, we must move out to grasp the opportunities that open to us. Of course this must be done with sensitivity and gentle care. Perhaps Hindu, Sikh or Moslem parents are preferring to send their children to the church schools rather than the state school (or, at times, even schools of their own faith) because its standards of discipline and morality are high. It is our responsibility to enable 'the least of these' to catch a glimpse of the glory of God, lived out by his people.

Jesus' deep concern for the whole person, his unwillingness to separate gospel and social action, his burden for the underside of society, need to be lived out by his church if that church is to survive. The burning question is how to translate that theory into practice in the local church.

'Our choice seems to be between sending a missionary and installing new carpet in the catacombs.'

THE WAY FORWARD

As we have seen, there are two aspects to mission: reaching out to the whole world evangelistically with the good news of Jesus, and reaching out with practical care and action on behalf of the hurting and marginalised in our society. Each area must be addressed if we are to be a thoroughly biblical church body (for God's sake!) and a thoroughly relevant church body (for the world's sake!).

As we reach out, the church must gain a new confidence

in its message. Do we really believe that Jesus Christ is the way to God? Do modern, materially successful men and women *need* him? Can't enlightened, sophisticated citizens of the twenty-first century do without him? Perhaps Jesus is only for certain types of people. Or perhaps he's just one of the meals on the menu in a world which offers Islam, Hinduism, Buddhism, and 'New-Age casserole' as dish of the day.

The church may have lost its confidence in itself in the face of stiff competition but it must regain its confidence in the message, if we are to have any hope of success in the aggressive market place where secular and religious systems display their wares. We need the confidence of Charles Spurgeon, who could testify, 'I have a great need for Christ; I have a great Christ for my need.' The supremacy and all-sufficient person of Jesus must be preached, believed and demonstrated among us again!

World mission

The risen Jesus sends the church into *the whole world* (Matthew 28:19). Many local churches have lost their global vision. And no wonder! Their only contact with missionary work has been through presentations which make reading the telephone directory seem appealing, from speakers who manage to look and sound like refugees from another century. Confidence has been lost in missionary work as secular bodies have criticised and dismissed it as paternalistic, even colonial or positively destructive. Some missionary societies make no effort to communicate their vision to the young people of today. With ageing leaderships and outdated structures all they can produce in many fellowships is a huge yawn. What a tragedy!

It need not be this way. There is growing recognition of the need to change, among both new and older established missionary agencies and to present their needs in a way that is lively and relevant, and will stimulate prayer, action and support.

Encourage involvement
We must encourage God's people to become involved in

missionary work if the church is to continue to grow, and there are steps we can take in support of missionary work both individually and as churches.

Individually we can:

- Visit another country to encourage a missionary.
- Use holiday time for some short-term missionary work.
- Buy books or attend a conference on missionary work.
- Set aside a regular sum of money for overseas mission.
- Receive a prayer letter from a missionary, and write regularly to them.
- Entertain a missionary on furlough; perhaps take them out for a meal or to the theatre.
- Subscribe to a missionary magazine.

The church can encourage this attitude in its members by setting aside time and money as a body to highlight missionary concerns.

As a church we could:

- Have a missionary Sunday with a difference – invite a variety of mission agencies to send their literature and display it attractively. In at least one of the services use a seminar style approach using drama, audio visuals, role play, etc. Encourage the congregation to ask questions. An interview can be as powerful as a sermon.
- Sponsor a trip to a missionary situation abroad. Encourage whoever goes to bring back a visual (slides/video) report as well as a verbal one.
- Adopt a missionary. Give financial support, pray, write and encourage. Make him or her your responsibility.
- Welcome returning missionaries with fanfares! Make them feel loved and honoured, but give them 'space' to re-acclimatise. Allow them to set the agenda for their furlough.
- Appoint a missionary 'rep' in the church whose job is to enthuse about specific mission projects and keep fresh information flowing to the leadership.
- Plan a mission evening around an appropriate meal (Chinese – pray for China, Indian – pray for India, Yorkshire pudding – pray for . . .). Perhaps have a non-European Christian (in his national costume?) give a testimony.

The challenge to personal commitment

One of the most important areas which we need to re-emphasise is the call to long-term missionary service. Christians at the end of the twentieth century need to be challenged about the possibility of a life-long commitment to serving God in another cultural setting. This is, of course, a very costly business. The price may well have to be paid in terms of family, friends, possessions and even health. But the world is desperate for such men and women. They are the kind of people who would respond to this description of the skills required for full-time workers in an advert which appeared in a Polynesian newspaper:

'Ability to mix with people, mix concrete, wade rivers write articles, love one's neighbour, deliver babies, sit cross-legged, drain swamps, digest questionable food, patch human weakness, suffer fools gladly and burn the midnight oil – these are required for service!

Persons allergic to ants, babies, beggars, chop suey, cock-roaches, curried crabs, duplicators, guitars, humidity, indif-ference, itches, jungles, mildew, minority groups, mud, poverty, sweat and unmarried mothers had better think twice before applying!'

This full-blooded appeal must be put to Christians again if the twenty-first century is to see missionaries of the calibre of William Carey (who arrived in India at the age of thirty-two and never left again, dying aged seventy-two!), C T Studd, Gladys Aylward, David Livingstone and Mary Slessor. The style of missionary activity has changed over the years; the need for a serious commitment to mission has not!

The 'home' mission-field

Christians have a major responsibility, not just to those in another country but to those in another kingdom – the king-dom of darkness. As we have noted many of the most despair-ing people in our world are those who find the gospel most irrelevant. Our record of identifying with the needy has not always been exemplary; often we are so absorbed in the 'niceties' of church life that blatant need goes unnoticed and, therefore, unmet. In this area as many others we are rearranging the deck-chairs while the Titanic sinks!

Take action
God must wonder when human suffering will touch the minds, emotions and wills of his children in a way that leads to action. I can feel the anguish behind John Steinbeck's questioning plea: 'Must the hunger become anger and the anger fury, before anything will be done?' And something must be *done*, both on the individual scale and the local church scale.

Individually, we can:

• Choose a simpler lifestyle. Plan to share resources with others in order to save money. Give what is saved to the needy.

• Open our homes to others. Are there ways in which we could be a 'family' to a lonely person? A homeless person? Someone on probation?

• Think through our attitudes to 'political' issues like unemployment, local government structures and finance, homelessness and the National Health Service. Make your views known to your MP and local councillors. Ask for prayer in church about these issues.

• Offer our time and/or gifts to help in a hostel for battered women, serve food at a 'soup kitchen', play with children at a school for the handicapped or visit a hospice.

• Go without food for a day or two (drink plenty of fluids and check with your doctor if you are concerned about this). Pray for the hungry as you do this. Perhaps you could send the money you save on food to help feed the starving.

• Be open to moving house to live in a more deprived part of our town or city. Then you could join that struggling inner city church.

• Do something! There really is 'enough for everyone's need, but not for everyone's greed'. Our small contribution can accomplish something; lots of small contributions can accomplish a great deal!

Local churches can make a difference to national issues. Decisions about, for example, abortion, overseas aid, pornography and racial discrimination have moral as well as political implications. It's not a question of whether the church has a right to speak or not on these matters – we have a *duty* not to keep silent! The unborn have no voice unless we speak for them. Many others have a 'quiet voice' easily drowned out by other priorities and pressure groups. We must speak out on their behalf or we risk sharing in society's guilt for inflicting pain upon them.

But how difficult this all is compared with preaching a 'simple' gospel message! Those outside the church will accuse us of 'dabbling in politics' and some of those inside the church will think we are being distracted from our primary calling. Certainly this mission-field is a mine-field. But didn't Jesus say things would get a little dangerous when people started living like his followers?! (See John 15:2–26; 16:33.)

Tactics
Some principles may help us through the mine-field.

● *Avoid being identified with a particular political party.* Some churches, by virtue of their location or the leanings of their leader, have adopted an agenda which closely mirrors a specific political grouping. This will make it very difficult for the church to be heard with respect by other political parties and very difficult for a Christian with a different political 'colour' to feel at home in the church. The other difficulty is that, almost unnoticed, the party manifesto becomes more influential than the Bible!

A church trying to be genuinely biblical will find itself at odds with each of the political parties from time to time. Inevitably, it will tend to be in confrontation with the 'ruling' party in local Government or the winner of a general election in national Government, because these groups have the power to effect change.

● *Be prayerful.* The spiritual dimension is what sets us apart from any other secular pressure group. No amount of letter writing, protest marching or lobbying can take the place of confronting the spiritual powers which lie behind so many 'political' problems. Only God's power can break Satan's grip on these parts of our society's life. Serious, intercessory prayer is our most potent political weapon.

● *Be positive.* Where possible, we need to have something to put in the place of what we are campaigning against! Where this is difficult, we should present our case peacefully and graciously. The officials of local or national Government are rarely *personally* to blame for the problem; they should be treated with respect and courtesy.

● *Be persistent.* There is a biblical precedent for being a 'godly nuisance' until justice is done (Luke 18:1–8). Write, phone, hold public meetings, lobby, whatever seems best. But don't give up easily. The walls of evil will fall down, but remember how many times it took to affect Jericho! Don't flit from one cause to another; only move on when the issue is resolved or you have done all you possibly can.

With these general guidelines it is possible to affect the community where you live and, with the support of others, affect the whole country. Or in words of the Lausanne Covenant, we can begin to share in being 'the whole church taking the whole gospel to the whole world'.

> Tell out, my soul,
>   the greatness of his might
> Powers and dominions
>   lay their glory by;
> Proud heart and stubborn wills
>   are put to flight,
> The hungry fed,
>   the humble lifted high.
>   © *Timothy Dudley-Smith*
>   *Reproduced by permission*

15

Into the Community

THE ISSUES

There are times when my wife's visionary idealism leaves me breathless. When we first met, she was involved with a missionary society, fired up by stories of Amy Carmichael, Hudson Taylor, C T Studd and others, with a vision to change the world. In time, that idealism has been tempered by realism, but the vision has never left her. Its focus has become clearer. Rather than change the entire world, the depth of her caring compassion has been expressed to individuals and has been used to bring many to wholeness.

During her formative teenage years, she lived in the slums of Sydney (now euphemistically called the 'inner-city'). Her father was the minister of a church there, and her mother would regularly find an alcoholic or homeless person sitting on the steps of the rectory asking for help. Cups of tea and chunky cheese sandwiches were the order of the day. It was a good introduction to getting hands dirty in community involvement. For her, it has always been a natural outworking of her faith.

So when we arrived in one of the parishes where we ministered, and there were plans afoot to upgrade the church hall, her visionary idealism, rooted in the community, came into full play. She imagined a multi-storey building providing housing for all sections of the community in need: those who were on their own because they were widowed, divorced, single or separated. There would be space for the homeless, who were increasing rapidly in number at that time. Professional carers would be on the spot to help with counselling and crisis management. Then there was to be provision for leisure and social activities – intergenerational of course. The nearby bag shop and jewellers could be converted into businesses that would be of more use to the community.

As we costed the venture, we thought: 'What's a few million dollars?' If our Father owned the cattle on a thousand hills, and owned the hills too, such an amount was not beyond him!

As it happened, the venture never materialised. But the principle was clear: if the church, any church, is to make inroads into the community, it needs to serve that community, to know it, and to respond to its needs.

Barriers between church and world

While the church remains inward-looking, or promotes a lifestyle that is inappropriate for the community in which it is placed, we will continue to send a mixed message, which is in danger of being misunderstood at best, and ignored at worst – the latter being the more likely alternative.

Lack of identification with the community

The Church of England (and other denominations too) own thousands of vast rectories designed for the days when rectory families of a dozen children were not uncommon. Even then, however, the message of comparative splendour such homes must have communicated to poor parishioners could have had only a damaging effect on the credibility of the gospel. Today, such houses are a nightmare to their occupants. Their size and age makes them impossible to heat and small clergy families find themselves rattling around in huge homes the wealthiest executive could ill afford. Is it appropriate? Does it help the church communicate the gospel with those around it?

The other side of the coin is the use Oscar Romero made of the archbishop's palace in El Salvador. With a commitment to the poor, he had the palace converted into a hospital, while he himself lived in a humble apartment in the shanty area of town. Which is the more appropriate model of the two, if the church's message is to be heard? Ronald Siders's motto, 'Live More Simply' may be a valid one for us all to emulate.

Lack of communication with the community

A further barrier between the church and the wider community is the feeling that the church is a secret society, with special language and customs, where 'outsiders' do not readily fit and are not really welcome. The closed (even locked) doors of the church make that message plain, as we saw in Chapter 6. The church must seem a strange world to those whose only links with it are the lampooning caricatures of the media, and baptisms, weddings and funerals.

So the basic problem would seem to be the separation of church and world or, more precisely, the belief that God is interested only in the 'religious' bits of life.

The people of Israel started off with a theocracy. God was their creator, leader, king, judge; all they ever did revolved around their relationship with him. Life and faith were inextricably intertwined. Even if they chose to disobey him, or to dabble with the syncretistic religions of their neighbours, they expected to suffer for it and pay the consequences.

Then they felt the need for human judges and kings, but God and their faith were still central to their lives. Society and community, individuals and families all belonged to God. Within the Israelite community there was no sense of 'them' and 'us' that is so common today (with phrases like 'Christians' and 'non-Christians', 'believers' and 'unbelievers', 'churchgoers' and 'non-churchgoers' all reflecting the tendency). It is only in recent times (particularly since the establishment of the state of Israel in 1948) that the concept of the 'secular Jew' has become so widely accepted. Even in the New Testament, with converts to the Way (as Christianity became known) from Judaism or the secular world, faith and life were all part and parcel of the one package. The community of the church, closely knit though it was, saw no separation between the life of faith and the life of their everyday world. They lived, laughed, wept and prayed together, in celebration and sorrow, in good times and bad. And although there were obvious lines of demarcation between those who were followers of Jesus and those who weren't, their integration into the community was not in question.

Then the church became structured. Hierarchy developed. And with Constantine's conversion, church and state became officially one. The irony is that what looked to be a blessing (the conversion of the Emperor himself) became a curse in disguise. Instead of church and society being integrated, the process of actual disintegration had begun. The increasing political power of the church was one of the root causes of the Dark Ages, when the light of the gospel was all but extinguished. Today, with all the advantages that are claimed for the Established church in England and certain Scandinavian countries, the perceived irrelevance of the church by the vast mass of its nominal adherents must surely raise serious questions.

'Excuse me. I'd like to volunteer for any ministry involving sensitivity and sacrifice in challenging a secularized, value-impoverished society with the radical claims of the gospel. I have Thursday afternoon free.'

Called to make a difference

Jesus used images that would have been striking to his hearers, to describe the functions of his followers:

> 'You are the salt of the earth ... You are the light of the world ... let your light shine before men, that they may see your good deeds and praise your Father in heaven.'
>
> *Matthew 5: 13–14, 16*

The people of God are meant to make a difference, in the community, to the community, through the community. How so? One of my memorable experiences was to share in a conference in Pattaya, Thailand. I was part of the 'large city' workshop, and a good deal of preparatory work was done prior to the conference. Ray Bakke led that part of the programme, which was an eye-opener to us all. Not only was he a walking encyclopaedia, with his mind stocked full of facts and figures about cities, from biblical, socio-economic, political and historical perspectives, but he made the concept of reaching cities for Christ an exciting adventure. What's more, he had a methodology that made sense. That same methodology, I believe, can apply equally to any community, however large or small, and whether urban, rural or suburban.

One of the first tasks, Ray suggested, for people taking community involvement seriously, is to work on a community profile. What categories of people are there in that particular community? Who are they? Where are they? When are they able to be contacted? What special features can we find out about them? What is their history? What is the breakdown of ages, income, language, racial background? What particular problems does the community face?

Such questions can be just starters for others that may well begin to flow once the exercise has begun. In downtown Chicago, where Ray and his family had lived for sixteen years at the time, fascinating stories and histories surfaced, opening up all kinds of possibilities for effective service to that particular community.

A similar exercise provided my wife's breathtaking, visionary idealism with ample challenge in the local church setting.

It was a seaside suburb, with a drifting population as well as settled older citizens, some of whom had lived there for fifty years or more. There was a thriving tourist trade, with the season of the year affecting who was around. There was an ageing population, but also homeless, unemployed, drug-taking street kids. The number of single parent families was high (thirty-two out of thirty-five children in one of the local primary school classes lived without both their natural parents). There were also large numbers of flat dwellers – or apartment dwellers, depending on the language! There were schools, a hospital, many hotels, sports and recreation clubs, the army base. The list of categories was almost endless.

Having identified the categories, how then to 'get our hands dirty', so to speak, and become really involved in the community? Looking back, it is still quite exciting to think what opportunities developed.

A tea room began for lonely shut-ins and became so popular it extended opening to four days a week. With a determination *not* to make it a typical fundraising effort, prices were kept to a minimum and quality kept high, and still hundreds of dollars came in for good causes. The proceeds were also to buy, for example, a bus for use by a home for elderly ladies. Support groups were begun for a wide range of targeted categories – women suffering from post-natal depression, bereaved, widowed, divorced, separated or single people, alcoholics. A professional counselling centre was established. Church members were encouraged to become involved in all aspects of community life, as candidates for local council elections (the youth worker from that time is now a candidate for mayor!), as involved members of all political parties, as committed members of school parents' and friends' associations. Neighbourhood cooperatives were formed, hospital visiting teams were formed and trained, and efforts made to serve the homeless and unemployed. A newspaper column was begun, so reaching the local community with a Christian perspective on events, and has been running ever since.

The church there was far from perfect. It still is, and always will be while it is composed of imperfect human beings. But it did have a profile and a credibility in the community. Doors opened for the gospel, and people who would otherwise have been unwilling to listen became ready to hear it.

If the church is not to close and die by the end of the decade, it has to 'be' Christ in the local community. What does this mean in practice? 'The word became flesh and lived for a while among us,' wrote John (John 1:14). That's what incarnation is all about. It's about living in the world, in society. It's about dirty hands. It's costly. It can be painful, unpleasant and thankless. It was for Jesus, as Paul makes abundantly clear, and it will be costly too for his church:

> '[Christ Jesus], being in very nature God,
>   did not consider equality with God
>   something to be grasped,
> but made himself nothing,
>   taking the very nature of a servant,
>   being made in human likeness.
> And being found in appearance as a man,
>   he humbled himself
>   and became obedient to death –
>   even death on a cross!'
>
> *Philippians 2: 6–8*

THE WAY FORWARD

Local churches are not simply preaching centres, and people are not just 'souls with ears'. We are becoming increasingly aware as Christians that people have social, emotional and physical needs as well as spiritual ones. A truly biblical church will want to tackle these issues, in addition to proclaiming the 'simple' message of repentance and faith. So local churches must get involved in the often difficult and costly work of caring for the community where they are: getting their hands dirty, loving people as people, not simply as potential pew-fodder! But how?

Know the needs

The first step is for the church to be convinced of the biblical call for this kind of community involvement. This is very clear in scripture and so churches don't usually take too much convincing – in theory! The theory only turns into practice when people become aware of the needs of others and of God's concern for them. Every individual is precious to God and each person's needs and concerns matter to him; when they matter to us too, we will be stirred into action.

Some time ago I received a letter from a lady in our church which describes some of the human pain which so moves God's heart. She movingly describes the hurt caused by a significant social issue – unemployment.

'Dear Stephen,

When you are unemployed you feel like a second- or third-class person. People do not accept that jobs are not around. You have to ask for everything you need as you cannot afford to buy things – like furniture. It is soul destroying. (Yes, it can make you think God doesn't care at times.) Your clothes are nearly always second-hand as new things are beyond your price reach. It is having to say to your children that what they want is too expensive or persuade them it is not very good and something a lot cheaper (often from a jumble sale) is much better. If you want to go on holiday you have to go begging to a charity for the money, also you cannot afford to go as a family or a couple again because of lack of money.

All this has been about the lack of money but that is just the start of it. The emotional side is far worse. I have to prop up the family when my husband has been around the factories and comes back with no job and says things like, "You would be better off if I left you or died." It is difficult to then talk about any problems I have, so they get buried and it becomes a vicious circle which reaches a point when you no longer talk to each other. The children do not get quality time from their father as the main interest becomes the TV and as he is always there it is always "later", but later never comes. You cannot have close friends as they cannot be invited over as you cannot offer a meal or anything.

Stephen, you said in the church magazine that there are people helping long-term unemployed but I do not know of any, unless you are talking about people who say, "I will pray for you." I do not mean to sound blasphemous but prayer is cheap. People expect you not to have things like washing machines, TVs, videos, radios. I do not know how little people expect us to live with or without. Maybe some would like to see us live under the stars and cook on an open fire eating berries we pick.

I am not sure what the Christian response should be but in this day and age of unemployment I know there must be one – if you know the answer let me know.

Stephen, I often feel it is the end of the line but I can always talk to God as there is no one else. I sometimes wonder what you would say to an IOU in the collection plate as sometimes there is nothing, not even 1p. in my purse on a Sunday. I sometimes think I will not go but I still turn up.

I hope this has not been too difficult to read.

God bless you and Janet,
Jesus is in charge.'

As churches are gripped by an understanding of how God feels about these damaged and wounded people, so genuine Christian social action becomes possible.

The ways this can be expressed are limitless. One of the churches in America most successful in 'community care' is in Denver, Colorado. Frank Tillapaugh, the pastor, says excitedly, 'To my joy, over these seventeen years, I've seen our church develop an outward focus. Currently we have twenty-five outreach ministries that target, for example, unwed mothers, jail inmates, international students, singles, the unchurched elderly and those in cults.' (*Leadership* Magazine, Summer 1988. Published by the Christianity Today Institute.) Of course, most local churches would be overwhelmed by this list! But it does at least show the kinds of things a fellowship *could* get involved with, if it was creative and imaginative.

How to start

The place to start is probably with a survey of the community. Two things need to be discovered: the needs of the community, and what provision already exists to meet those needs. These facts can be discovered by a series of interviews with key people in the community and by a random survey of views from the community as a whole. When we did this for our own church, we broke the interviews into three sections:

PROFESSIONAL INTERVIEWS

1 Headteachers/staff/welfare workers at all the main educational establishments.
2 Doctors and health visitors.
3 Ministers of all the churches.

ORGANISATIONAL INTERVIEWS

1 Statutory bodies:
- Police
- Social Services

2 Non-statutory bodies:
- Samaritans
- Family Network
- Relate
- Council on Alcoholism

COMMUNITY INTERVIEWS

1 Publicans
2 Recreation Centre staff
3 Shopkeepers
4 Random door knocking – with questionnaire

These three categories kept one person occupied, full-time, for a month! The resulting report, which also attempted to draw some conclusions from the data discovered, ran to forty-three pages plus a twenty-two page appendix! Never before had we had such accurate information about our community. Thankfully, the report confirmed what we had suspected – but now we could prove it. This 'high-quality' information led to much more carefully targeted prayer, various new emphases in outreach and ultimately to the appointment of a full time social worker.

None of this happened quickly, but the survey gave the impetus for change to begin. We began with very little expertise and developed more significant programmes as time went on, and our confidence and skill grew.

Local churches can also draw on the support of care organisations (we are in a joint project with Spurgeon's Child Care) who are delighted to give professional advice and help. When you have completed a survey it would be valuable to contact one of these organisations to see where they feel the *priorities* are in the list of needs your survey has revealed. This link will protect churches from embarking on some well-intentioned project which appears valuable, but in fact is ineffective or even counter-productive. More than one church has initiated a project to meet a particular need, only to find itself swamped with the needy and unable to cope. When the project folds up prematurely the needy individuals are hurt, the congregation disillusioned and the church/community relations are strained. This is why it is so vital to survey thoroughly for accurate information about the community; to progress slowly and thoughtfully; and to consult other agencies for their input.

Some early steps in social action could be:

• Give time once a month in a Sunday service to pray about a particular community need.

• Send a gift of money to a local home for the elderly or school for the handicapped.

• Arrange a car rota to take shut-ins or disabled people shopping or to church.

• Have a 'community care' Sunday, when local doctors, police or social workers can be invited to church. Special prayers can be said for their work.

• Plan a community lunch, to which the isolated and immobile can be brought. Serve a hot meal; perhaps have some community singing.

• Run a 'parents and toddlers' group. If possible have a good-as-new stall at the same time, where inexpensive children's clothes can be bought.

• Order a regular copy of the magazine of a Christian community care organisation.

Collect resources

The church can also fulfil a valuable role as a 'clearing house' for social care. That is, we can guide people to those who can help them best, without needing to possess the expertise ourselves. We can do this by collecting resources under three categories:

1 Local Christians.

Make a list of people in your church who would be willing to act as 'contact points'. This list would include members of the caring professions and those with specific abilities in specialist areas, such as accountants, lawyers and teachers. Debt is a huge problem in our society. Don't forget to include a number of mature people who are good at listening – lots of issues find some resolution when shared with a sympathetic ear!

It may also be possible to tap into the resources of other local churches, who will have people with different skills and qualifications.

2 List of local resources.

This should include the hospital, police, fire brigade and social services. In addition, list a wide cross-section of voluntary care agencies operating in your area, for instance Gamblers Anonymous, Samaritans, Age Concern and Relate; plus all the support groups for drug abusers, single parents, and so on. (If you have a list of less than thirty, you have missed an important group!)

3 Collect samples of literature.

Free leaflets from government agencies, local statutory bodies and care organisations are available on everything from AIDS to youth employment schemes. Read the information carefully to make sure involvement with them will not compromise the church in some way, but you will usually find that they contain simple, factual information which is practical and helpful.

By making these three categories of resource available, we can provide an excellent service to those both inside and outside the church. A small team of people can be responsible for keeping the lists up to date and could also assist the leaders of the church in referring those in need to the most appropriate person or organisation. This is a particularly valuable service because in many communities there is a significant amount of help available, but hardly anyone knows it's there!

All of these things help us to fulfil the great commission in its broadest biblical terms. Caring for the wounded and the struggling in our localities, in the name of Christ; bringing the message of Jesus with the compassion of Jesus. Only this 'full-orbed' ministry accurately reflects the scriptural material and adequately expresses God's heart of love.

> 'Make me a channel of your peace:
> where there's despair in life let me bring hope,
> where there is darkness, only light,
> and where there's sadness, ever joy:
>> O Master grant that I may never seek
>> so much to be consoled as to console;
>> to be understood as to understand,
>> to be loved, as to love with all my soul!'

And so, we hope the title of our book is obvious in its negative implications. We want to see Christ's church becoming what God intended her to be in the next decade. We don't want to see her as an irrelevant, archaic, marginalised, dying relic of ancient times. We long to see new life and growth, and we pray that God's will might be done in her, and through her on earth, as it is in heaven. And to God be the glory.

RESOURCE BOOKS AND ORGANISATIONS

1 A divided church

Amess, Robert. *One in the Truth*. Eastbourne: Kingsway, 1988.

Gundry, Patricia. *Heirs Together: Mutual Submission in Marriage*. Grand Rapids: Zondervan, 1980.

Gundry, Patricia. *Neither Slave nor Free: Helping Women Answer the Call to Church Leadership*. New York: Harper & Row, 1987.

Gundry, Patricia. *Woman Be Free!* Grand Rapids: Zondervan, 1977.

Hull Gretchen Gaebelein. *Equal to Serve: Women and Men in the Church and Home*. London: Scripture Union, 1989.

Swartley, Willard. *Slavery, Sabbath, War and Women*. Scottdale: Herald Press, 1983.

2 Better together

Cormack, David. *Team Spirit: People Working With People*. London: MARC Europe, 1987.

Griffiths, Michael. *Get Your Act Together, Cinderella: Call to the Church of Today*. Leicester: IVP, 1989.

Sheppard, David and Worlock, Derek J. *Better Together: Christian Partnership in a Hurt City*. London: Hodder, 1988.

The Evangelical Alliance: exists to promote unity and co-operation among evangelical churches and organisations, and to provide services to them. Whitefield House, 186 Kennington Park Road, London SE11 4BT. Also at: The Salt Cellar, 65 The Shopping City, Runcorn, Cheshire, WA7 2BX.

3 Leadership

Beasley-Murray, Paul. *Dynamic Leadership: Making it Work for You and Your Church*. Eastbourne: Monarch Publications, 1990.

Gibbs, Eddie. *Followed or Pushed? Understanding and Leading Your Church*. Bromley: MARC Europe, 1987.

4 Administration: Getting it done

Brierley, Peter W. *Vision Building: Knowing Where You're Going*. London: Hodder, 1989.

Handy, Charles. *The Age of Unreason*. London: Arrow Books, 1990.

MacDonald, Gordon. *Ordering Your Private World*. Crowborough: Highland Books, 1987.

Administry: runs many practical and imaginative training courses to equip church workers in church administration. 69 Sandridge Road, St Albans, Hertfordshire, AL1 4AG.

Marc Europe: runs day and residential courses in management, based on biblical principles, for Christian leaders. Cosmos House, 6 Homesdale Road, Bromley, Kent BR2 9EX.

5 Going for growth

Brierley, Peter. *Christian England: Results of the 1989 English Church Census*. London: MARC Europe, 1991.

Cleverly, Charlie. *Church Planting: Our Future Hope*. London: Scripture Union, 1991.

Gibbs, Eddie. *I Believe in Church Growth* (2nd ed). London: Hodder, 1990.

British Church Growth Association: exists to share church growth interests, insights and experience throughout the UK. It undertakes research, teaching, consultancy and runs church growth conferences. St Mark's Chambers, Kennington Park Road, London SE11 4PW.

6 Communication

Rye, James. *The Communicator's Craft: Getting Your Message Across*. Leicester: IVP, 1990.

7 Getting the Message

Fee, Gordon and Stuart, Douglas. *How to Read the Bible for all its worth*. London: Scripture Union, 1988.

Gaukroger and Mercer. *Frogs in Cream*. London: Scripture Union, 1991.

Hybels, Bill. *Mastering Contemporary Preaching*. Leicester: IVP, 1991.

Robinson, Haddon W. *Expository Preaching: Principles and Practice*. Leicester: IVP. 1986.

White, John, and others. *Hear the Word: Encountering its Life*. Leicester: IVP, 1990.

8 Small Groups in the Church

Mallison, John. *Growing Christians in Small Groups*. London: Scripture Union, 1989.

Peace, Richard. *Small Group Evangelism*. London: Scripture Union, 1987.

Pointer, Roy (Foreword). *Good Things Come in Small Groups*. Scripture Union, 1987.

Walker, Tom. *Small Streams, Big Rivers*. London: Scripture Union, 1991.

9 Training in the Church

Baumohl, Anton. *Grow Your Own Leaders*. London: Scripture Union, 1987.

Crix, Frederick. *Taking a Lead: A Practical Guide to Leadership Roles in Your Church*, London: Scripture Union, 1991.

Scripture Union National Training Centre: is the largest interdenominational training agency in Britain. It runs training courses on a wide variety of subjects for churches and Christian groups –

for ministers, elders, deacons, house-group leaders, social workers, community health workers, youth and children's workers, committee members, etc. Scripture Union National Training Centre, 26–30 Heathcoat Street, Nottingham, NG1 3AA.

10 A Church for the Family

Bridger, Francis. *Children Finding Faith*. London: Scripture Union, 1988.

Buckland, Ron. *Children and God*. London: Scripture Union, 1988.

Crawford, Kathleen. *Under-fives Welcome!* London: Scripture Union, 1990.

Graystone, Peter. *Help! There's a Child in my Church!* London, Scripture Union, 1989.

Learning All Together: A quarterly resource magazine for ministers and other church leaders. Includes weekly resource material for all-age worship, all-age talks, adult sermons, adult group material, articles for use as discussion starters or in a church magazine, book reviews, etc. Published by Scripture Union.

Leonard, Joe. *Family Ministry*. London: Scripture Union, 1988.

11 Pastoral Care

Collins, Gary. *Christian Counselling: A Comprehensive Guide*. Milton Keynes: Word Publishing, 1989.

Hurding, Roger. *Roots and Shoots*. London: Hodder, 1986.

Tidball, Derek. *Skilful Shepherds*. Leicester: IVP, 1986.

White, R E O *Guide to Pastoral Care*. London: Pickering and Inglis, 1979.

12 Commitment

Foster, Richard. *Celebration of Discipline*. London: Hodder, 1983.

Macdonald, Gordon. *Rebuilding Your Broken World*. Crowborough: Highland Books, 1988.

MacDonald, Gordon. *Restoring Your Spiritual Passion*. Crowborough: Highland Books, 1989.

Swindoll, Charles. *The Grace Awakening*. Milton Keynes: Word, 1990.

Kendall, RT. *Tithing*. London: Hodder, 1992.

13 Evangelism: Do or die!

Gaukroger, Stephen, *It Makes Sense*. London: Scripture Union, 1987.

Green, Michael. *Evangelism in the Early Church*. Crowborough: Highland Books, 1984.

Green, Michael. *Evangelism through the Local Church*. London:

Hodder & Stoughton, 1990.

British Youth for Christ: is involved in evangelistic outreach to young people, through church-based missions, school work, community involvement and training. Cleobury Place, Cleobury Mortimer, Kidderminster, Worcestershire DY14 8JG.

Saltmine Trust: is involved in evangelism, teaching and training at home and overseas, at the invitation of church fellowships. PO Box 15, Dudley, West Midlands DY3 2AN.

14 Mission

Egner, Malcolm. *Mission: Possible.* London: Scripture Union, 1990.

Samuel, Vinay and Sugden, Chris. *Evangelism and the Poor: A Third World Study Guide.* Oxford: Regnum Books, 1982.

Sookhdeo, Patrick (ed). *Sharing Good News.* London: Scripture Union, 1991.

Evangelical Missionary Alliance: encourages co-operation, and provides co-ordination, between missionary societies, churches and colleges. Whitefield House, 186 Kennington Park Road, London SE11 4BT.

15 Into the Community

Frontier Youth Trust: trains and provides help for Christians working with alienated young people, mainly in urban/industrial areas. 'Envisions' churches for this work and runs camps for young people. Scripture Union House, 130 City Road, London EC1V 2NJ.

Spurgeon's Childcare: supports families under stress, keeps them together, aims to give help before children are taken into care. 30 Mill Street, Bedford MK40 3HD.